THE EASY PEASY METHOD
For
WRITING
MEMOIRS & FAMILY
Stories

RANDY LINDSAY

Write House Publishing

ISBN 978-1-952040-04-7

Contents

INTRODUCTION

D o you have a story you want to tell?

A story about a larger-than-life ancestor that needs to be told before it's forgotten. Details about a family line that might help genealogy researchers connect to their past. Maybe you want to tell the world about the amazing experiences you've shared with your close family. Or, perhaps something has happened in your life that might allow others to learn from your experience.

The longer you think about it, chances are good you have at least one story that needs to be told. Memoirs and family history stories allow us to leave important lessons to future generations. When we tell these stories, our ancestors are kept alive in our memories.

But those stories do nothing unless someone reads them. If your book is dull, it will sit on a shelf and gather dust. No family history is interesting until someone makes it interesting. Before that happens, the information gathered about your family is just a bunch of names, places, and numbers. Most people don't want to plow through a mountain of data. They want to read a story. Family historians and memoir writers can benefit by taking a few storytelling tips from fiction authors.

The Easy-Peasy Method is meant to help you turn dry facts into something people will be excited to read. It will teach you how to interview friends and family and discover the interesting details of their lives. Then once you have a collection of stories, this book will help you decide which ones to write and how to write them. Maybe you're thinking—

I'm Not a Writer.

That's alright. This book isn't meant for writers. The Easy-Peasy Method is for average people who want to tell stories about themselves, or their family, in a way that will be fun to read, as well as educational. And best of all, this book is designed to explain each step in a way that makes sense to the average person.

I Don't Want to Write a Full-Length Book.

No problem. Stories come in all sizes. No matter what size story you want to write, the Easy-Peasy Method can help you. The ideas in this book work for:

- Stories only a few pages long.

- Short stories.

- Booklet-sized stories.

- Stories the length of a full-blown novel.

I'm Not Writing a Story for Anyone Else.

Once again, the Easy-Peasy Method can help you. The methods described in this book provide help for any story. These tips will help if you want to:

- Write a story for yourself.

- Write a story for your family.

- Write a story for family historians.

- Write a story for people who are in the same situation as you.

- Write a story for publication.

Interest in writing memoirs and family histories is growing, but most people hesitate simply because they don't know how. They're not even sure where to start the process. All those precious memories sit inside them, bubbling up, waiting to be told. And if the person dies before they find a way to express themselves . . . those memories are lost.

There's no reason to wait any longer. The Easy-Peasy Method is split into sections designed to guide you through the writing process one topic at a time. Learn the first-step in writing your story. Then discover how to interview people to find their stories. Find out how to create a storyline. Learn which events make for an interesting story, how to use historic details to bring your story to life, and how to put tension into your story. All of these methods are explained in a way that's easy to understand.

Let's get started.

WHAT DO YOU WANT TO WRITE?

The idea of writing a memoir, or family story, can feel overwhelming if you don't know where to start. A lot of elements go into writing a good story. Decisions about what events to write about, where to begin the story, and which details to use aren't difficult if you start the right way.

Where do you start? That's easy, by deciding which story you want to write. Everything is affected by your choice of story. That's the first-step and this chapter will guide you in deciding what story you want to tell.

MANY STORIES

It doesn't matter if you're writing a memoir or a story about your family because each of our lives are filled with dozens of interesting events. There won't be one single story to tell, rather there will be the story you decide to tell. As we work through the process of finding which story you're going to tell, don't overthink your decisions. Don't stress about which story you begin with, or whether your choices are wrong, because there are no wrong answers. There are only possibilities.

If you work through this process a dozen times, you might end up with a dozen different stories. And that's alright. Each story has value. And don't worry about leaving out a portion of the person's life. No book can contain every event that has happened in a person's life. You are telling one story, not all stories about that person.

STORY GUIDE

The Easy-Peasy Story Guide is a tool to help find the story you want to tell. Or, at least, the story you want to tell at this time. The story guide contains a series of questions to determine how your story should be written and what elements it should contain. Detailed explanations of how to use these questions to write your story are given later in the book. For now, just concentrate on filling out the story guide.

You can find a blank story guide at the end of the chapter. Feel free to make a copy of the page or download one from:

www.easypeasymethod.com/memoir-resource

You might want to print it out on card stock and keep it with you as you write your story. The story guide will remind you of the story you decided to write at the beginning of the process.

Randy Lindsay

Memoir vs. Family Chronicle

The first step in writing a family history story, or memoir, is to decide what you want to write. If the book is about you, then you want to write a memoir. A story about either your living relatives or your ancestors would be a family chronicle.

Plenty of terms exist to describe the kind of story you might tell. They include personal memoirs, family biographies, multi-generational stories, and family history memoirs. Each of those terms describe a specific kind of story, but why complicate the matter? The book will be about you . . . or your family. That makes it either a memoir or a family chronicle.[1] Easy-peasy.

Example: *The Milkman's Son* is about the author. That makes it a memoir.

> ## Pull out your Story Guide.
> ## Record your choice on the
> ## Memoir vs. Family Chronicle line.

---

1 Why call it a family chronicle instead of a family story? Because memoirs, family chronicles, short stories, and any other kind of historic tale you can think of are all stories. Rather than confuse the reader with too many uses of the word, we are just going to refer to the longer family history stories as family chronicles. Besides, family chronicle sounds way more interesting than family history story.

Scrapbooks, Anthologies, and Family Chronicles

Next, you will want to decide the best way to tell the story. Once again, there are plenty of options, too many, in fact. Rather than sort through a confusing list of minor differences, let's break it down in to three easy categories: Scrapbooks, Anthologies, and Family Chronicles.

Here's a quick explanation about these three types of stories. A scrapbook is a collection of pictures with just enough story details to tell the reader about the images. An anthology is a collection of short stories that are normally based on a theme. And a family chronicle is one continuous story. Family chronicles can be as short as a few pages or as long as a full-length book.

Any of these three styles can be used to tell your story. A memoir can be a scrapbook, an anthology, or a family chronicle. Each style has its advantages and will create a different kind of story from the others. Choose the style that best fits the kind of story you want to tell. If you have a lot of pictures of yourself and want to limit the amount of writing you do, then write your memoir as a scrapbook. Or if you are writing about one of your ancestors and want it to read more like a novel, then go with the family chronicle option.

If you're not sure which style to pick, you can come back to this choice later. It may help for you to go through the rest of the decisions about the kind of story you want to write before you make this one. You could even write three versions of the story and decide which style works best. Maybe not three whole stories—just the first few pages of each.

Example: *The Milkman's Son* is one continuous story. That makes it a chronicle.

> Record your choice on the Scrapbooks, Anthologies & Family Chronicle line of the Story Guide.

Who Are You Writing About?

If you are writing a memoir, it might seem like the obvious answer is you're writing about . . . YOU! But, in this case, which part of you is the story about? A person who served in the military and fought in a war is telling a different story than the person who battled cancer. Even if both of those people are you, each of those are different stories. A specific story will have a different feel and offer distinct messages to the reader.

Think of yourself as several people inside the same body. If you are telling the story about you as a soldier, use only those elements that are important to being a soldier. Do your best to think like you did during that part of your life and write what you felt at that time. Find the questions that work best for a soldier's story. Then answer those questions as a soldier.

Stories don't have to be about just one person, especially, when you are dealing with family history. A story might be about an entire family or even several generations. Decide whether you want to write about one individual, a single family, multiple families, or a multi-generational family. However, keep in mind that the more people you include in the story, the less can be written about any one of them.

But, if you are working on a family history, then you may want to include several or even many people. The story could be done as a single line of descendants from one of your ancestors. It could include all the descendants from a married couple. It could be about all of the families who lived in a specific place at a specific time. Or maybe you only want to write about your grandparents.

Example: *The Milkman's Son* is about the time in the author's life when he discovered that his dad was not his biological father and that he had an entire family he didn't know.

> Record your choice on the
> Who Are You Writing About
> line of the Story Guide.

What Do You Want Your Audience to Know About This Person?

Now, that you know who you want to write about, you need to decide what it is you want people to know about that person, or family, or families. Did they do something important, newsworthy, or historically significant? Do you just want people to know the kind of life they lead? Or do you want to show how the events of their lives had an impact on the lives of later generations? Keep in mind that these are family stories. It is perfectly okay if all you want to do is make sure that the people you write about have their lives remembered.

Example: *The Milkman's Son* was about letting people know what it was like to discover unknown family members.

> Record your choice on the
> **What Do You Want Your Audience to Know** line of the Story Guide.

Why Are You Writing It?

What makes you want to write this story? Why do you want to write about this person, or group of people? Why is it important to share this story? Keeping in mind the reason why you want to write a story will help you to decide which ideas and events to include in the book. It will help you put together the information you write about in a manner that will make the most sense.

Remember, there are no wrong answers to this question, or any of the questions in this book. All of the questions in this book are designed to help narrow the amount of information you will use in your story. As you collect memories and historical data about the events of the person's life, knowing the answer to your purpose for writing the story will allow you to decide which bits fit together and which ones don't.

If you're not sure why you want to write a memoir or family story you can take a look at the list below and pick one that seems to fit best with what you have in mind.

- You want to make sure the person or people in your story are not forgotten.

- The person or people in your story did something important that can help others.

- You want to leave a legacy for your family.

- You want to grow closer to an older generation by learning and sharing their stories.

- You love the interesting stories you have heard and want to share them.

- Each life touches the lives of others and you want to share some of those stories.

- You want to turn the abstract details of family history into something fun and personal.

- You want to record stories before the memory of them become distorted or even lost.

- You want to leave a detailed record for others researching your family lines.

- You want to build on your sense of family.

- You want to write about others because you want to understand them better.

- You hope your story will encourage others to write about the same person or people.

Example: *The Milkman's Son* was written in the hope that people would read it and then be willing to take a chance on reaching out to lost family members.

Record your choice on the Why Are You Writing This Story line in the Story Guide.

Who Are Your Readers?

Who do you expect to read your book? Your grandchildren? Members of the extended family? Family history researchers? Or do you think this will be a story that many people will find interesting, family and non-family alike? You can also ask yourself, "What kind of person will benefit from this story?"

It's important to keep your audience in mind while writing the book. If it's being written for family members who may have never met the person the book is about, then you will want to include plenty of details that will paint a picture of the person in the readers minds. If it's being written for the benefit of anyone doing family history research, then you will want to make sure all of the usual statistics are included with the story. A younger audience will need a story that is easier to understand. An audience that is going through the same trials as the person you are writing about will want as many details about that event, or experience, as possible.

This might sound difficult, but all you have to do is ask yourself, "Is what I'm about to write, something I think my readers will find interesting or helpful?" The more you practice writing for your audience, the more interesting the story will be for them.

Example: *The Milkman's Son* was written for anyone who has discovered unknown family members through DNA testing. Or anyone who knows someone close to them that has had that same experience.

> ## Record your choice on the
> ## Who Are Your Readers
> ## line of the Story Guide.

What Tone Do You Want?

Do you want to make readers laugh? Or is the story you're writing more serious? A good story has a mix of emotions. Dramas often have funny, or romantic, parts to lighten the mood before the next dramatic scene. Great comedies have serious moments in them. You don't have to write with a specific tone in mind, but the story will be better if you do.

Knowing the tone of your book can help you decide what kind of events to include in the story. It can even help you pick which words to use. A serious story about how a person overcame an addiction can include all sorts of words that remind the reader of the emotional struggle of that situation.

If you don't already know what sort of tone you want the book to have, the easiest way to decide this is to look at how you answered, "Why are you writing this book?"

Example: *The Milkman's Son* has a light-hearted and often humorous tone. This was meant to show the personality of the author and add to the message of hope that was intended.

> ## Record your choice on the
> ## What Tone Do You Want
> ## line of the Story Guide.

What message do you want to share with your readers?

Earlier in the chapter, you decided why you wanted to write a book. The answer to that question helps you to know what events and information belong in the story. But you also want to know the best way to tell the story to the reader.

Ask yourself, "What message do I want people to know?" The answer can be as simple as Grandpa Jones helped everyone who needed assistance. If you choose a message you feel strongly about, the chances are good the reader will feel it too.

The message you choose can help to determine which emotions are appropriate for the story and how you want the people in the story to respond to the events that take place. Your message will determine the perspective that is used throughout the story. The message you want to share with others is the theme of the story, affecting all elements of what you write.

Example: *The Milkman's Son* wanted to share the message that the benefits of meeting lost family members was worth taking the risk of rejection. That by knowing our family we know more about ourselves.

Record your choice on the
What Message
Do You Want to Share
line of the Story Guide.

You Said This Would Be Easy!

Don't panic.

This chapter has mentioned a lot of writing concepts all at once. If you were expected to remember everything in the chapter, then The Easy-Peasy Method of Writing Memoirs and Family Stories wouldn't be easy. But you don't have to remember all of the writing concepts in this chapter or even use them. Just relax and keep learning.

The purpose of the Easy-Peasy Story Guide is to help you decide what to include in your story and how to tell it. Knowing what you want to write about will keep you from wandering away from the story you want to tell. The Easy-Peasy Story Guide gives you the basic answers that will make the actual writing of the story easier.

By filling out the Easy-Peasy Story Guide, you have started the work on your memoir, or family story. You have taken the first step in writing your story and that's the hardest part of the process. And most importantly, you are now past the stage of wondering where to start.

Keep the Easy-Peasy Story Guide as a reminder of the decisions you made about your story. You might even want to print it out on card stock and place it next to you when you write. Not only will it serve as a reminder of which story you set out to tell, but it will also make it easy to see which ideas you want to use during your current writing session.

EASY-PEASY STORY GUIDE

Are you writing a memoir or a family chronicle?

What format do you want to use for this story? (Scrapbook, Anthology, Family Chronicle)

Who are you writing about? (Person, Family, Ancestral Line)

What do you want your audience to know about this person?

Why are you writing this story?

Who are your readers?

What tone do you want for your story?

What message do you want to share with your readers?

NOTES

NOTES

SCRAPBOOKS AND ANTHOLOGIES

S crapbooks and anthologies are an easier method of writing memoirs and family stories than the longer family chronicle style. Both also benefit greatly from the use of themes and have been put into the same chapter for that reason. If this is your first attempt to write a book, it might be better to start with one of these two styles and leave the longer family chronicle for your next project.

Before going any further, make sure your Easy-Peasy Story Guide is within reach. The decisions you made when planning your story will make the rest of the writing process easier. And that's what this book is all about, making it as easy as possible to write about you and your family.

THEME

Themes for scrapbooks and anthologies are different from the themes you might use for longer stories. Scrapbook and anthology themes are more like party themes. They're a fun way to connect the pictures or short stories to one another.

The theme is also going to replace the need to plot a storyline, which you would use for a family chronicle. Instead, you will use the theme to choose which pictures and short stories belong together. Pictures and stories that don't fit the theme will distract readers from the message you want to tell them.

Take a look at your Easy-Peasy Story Guide. "Why are you writing this story?" and "What message do you want to share with readers?" are both great questions to help you decide on your theme.

For example, you might have family who lived in another country. The answer to the above questions could be that you want readers to know what it was like for your family to live there and maybe even why they moved. The theme for either a scrapbook or anthology based on those answers might be described as, "The Lindsays in Ireland." All of the pictures or stories would be about your family living in that country.

Fun themes can be used if your goal is to just let readers know what your family is like in a more general sense. Here are a few themes to consider:

> **Holidays** – each chapter can be about a specific holiday. Start with New Years and work your way through to the end of December. Keep in mind that the purpose is to give the readers a glimpse of what holiday life was like for your family. Instead of focusing on all of the holidays you can pick one and show how the traditions changed over the course of many years. Or maybe you want to make this an extended family project and show how all of your grandparents, siblings, and cousins celebrate the holiday. There are an endless number of ways to put together a holiday theme scrapbook or anthology.

Food – most family events center around food. A scrapbook or anthology that uses food for its theme can include a story about an individual or family, a small interview, and a recipe for their favorite meal. The book can be grouped by family units, holidays, or any other category that comes to mind.

Favorite Activities – like the food theme, a scrapbook or anthology can include stories from individuals about their favorite thing to do. Favorite family activities have the advantage of being interesting to more readers as well as telling a story about a group rather than a single person. If you collect stories from the other people who participated in the activity you can make a book about a single spectacular event.

Memorials – if a loved one has passed away, memories about that person make a great theme for a book that can be shared with the entire family. Post pictures of individuals when they were with the lost family member. Include some memories or stories everyone has about the events shown in the picture.

Family – this theme can be based on a single family. Chapters can progress from the time when Mom and Dad dated and then move to the present day. Each chapter can be about someone in the family or they can be based on important events.

Travel – for this theme, you will want to bring out the family's vacation pictures or stories. Show and tell your readers about all the interesting places you went and all the fun and not-so-fun activities you did while on those trips. Each family member can pick their favorite part of a trip and write a short description and why they liked it. Or, if you prefer a more realistic take on your travels, have everyone talk about the worst part of the trip.

Business – scrapbooks and anthologies don't have to be all fun and games. You or members of your family may have made wonderful contributions to the business world. Innovations in an industry or a lifelong commitment to a company should be shared with others.

The Big Event – sometimes a single event has a greater impact on a family than a lifetime of smaller ones. This could be a move by a post-Civil War family in the south to the wilds of the American West. Or it could be how a family dealt with the devastating effects of a natural disaster. If you are writing to have your story picked-up by a publisher, you will want to write about a Big Event. Publishers want Big Event stories.

Here's a list of other ideas:

- Awards and Presentations
- Favorite Things
- Family Hobbies
- Sports
- Family Talents
- Pets
- Dreams/Passions/Goals
- Favorite Moments

SCRAPBOOKS

If you have a lot of pictures, a scrapbook is the easiest way to create a family story. A scrapbook will mean less writing for you and less reading for your audience. Not only will readers will be less intimidated reading a scrapbook, but the highly visual nature of the book makes it more fun to read. This is good, because it can be a challenge to convince people to read a book about family history.

Scrapbooks have disadvantages as well. The stories in a scrapbook tend to be on the skimpy side, making this kind of book a poor choice for describing events that really need a detailed and in-depth approach. Scrapbooks require a lot of pictures. If you don't have enough pictures, then you should consider writing an anthology or a family chronicle.

Divide and Conquer

Books are usually divided into smaller sections called chapters. This makes a story easier to write because you're only working on one small part at a time. If you focus on a single chapter while you work, rather than what it takes to complete the entire book, then the project feels doable. And the less stress you feel, the more you can concentrate on writing.

The first step for a scrapbook is to separate the pictures into groups. All of the pictures in a group should have something in common—an element that connects them. The pictures could be grouped by families or individuals, chronologically, by location, or anything that makes sense to you.

Once you have the pictures grouped together, start working on the chapters. Order the pictures in a way that tells a story. That might be from the oldest to the newest picture, but there are as many ways to layout the order of the pictures as there are people who want to put together a scrapbook. Be creative. Show your personality as you create your chapters.

Tell yourself a story as you put the pictures in order. What do you remember about the events that took place in those pictures? Describe those events out loud and see if a story doesn't form in your mind. Then place the pictures in the order they appear in your story.

It's a good idea to record yourself as you tell these stories. That way you won't have to worry about writing down what you said during your storytelling session. Your thoughts, or memories, will flow out of you without interruption, leaving you with a heart-felt story.

Easy-peasy.

More Than Pictures

A scrapbook story is more than just a bunch of pictures. It still needs words to convey the message you want to tell to the reader. Without bits of story from you, a scrapbook is only a collection of pictures that have no meaning to the audience. But writing something to go with your pictures doesn't have to be hard.

Start With A Story

As strange as this might seem, the story you tell in each chapter starts with the title. It's best to avoid giving each chapter a title based on the number in which it appears in the book. Tell your audience what the chapter is about. If it about Josh's eleventh birthday? Then title it, "Happy Eleventh Birthday, Josh." Or how about, "Eleven and Loving It."

As soon as your audience reads the chapter title, expectations form in their minds and the story is already underway. They may be curious about what the title means and want to read the chapter because of that. At the very least, the title has given the reader an idea of what might be in the chapter and they will be drawn into reading it to see if the story plays out the way they thought it might.

That doesn't mean you have to decide on a title before you write the story. It only means that the story actually starts with the title. Spend a little time thinking of an appropriate title, one that will immediately plunge the reader into the story.

In addition to the title, at the beginning of each chapter, you will want to add a few paragraphs, or even a whole page, to explain what the pictures are about. This is a mini-story. Make sure to include some thoughts, emotions, and observations you might have about the events that take place in the pictures. Your audience will appreciate the personal touch you give the book with your comments.

For example, if the pictures in the chapter are from when you lived in a specific home, then you might want to write something like this:

We lived in the house on 31st Avenue for more than ten years. It was longer than we lived in any other house during my childhood. We started on the east side of Phoenix and each move seemed to take us farther west. We stayed in this neighborhood long enough to see a lot of major changes. The area looked very different by the time we moved out. I attended most of grade school and all of high school while living in this house and most of my childhood memories are associated with it.

Pictures + Statistics Does Not = An Interesting Story.

Putting the names, places, and dates below a picture is not enough. Your audience will quickly grow tired of pictures and facts alone. But you can make your pictures more interesting by attaching a Three-Sentence Story to each of them.

Adding a Three-Sentence Story to each of the pictures will not only make your scrapbook more fun to read, it's also a great way to practice your storytelling skills. You may want to consider starting with a scrapbook, or two, before attempting a book that requires quite a bit more writing to tell the story.

THE THREE-SENTENCE STORY

All stories have a beginning, a middle, and an end.

This is such an important concept in storytelling that I'm going to repeat it. ALL stories have a beginning, a middle, and an end. Long stories. Short stories. Somewhere in the middle stories. All of them are divided into the same parts.

These three sections create the basic structure of a story. Each part serves a specific function. It's easier to write a story if you know what each of these sections are meant to do and what story elements should be placed in each of them. And knowing where everything goes is the biggest challenge in writing a story.

Each sentence in a Three-Sentence Story represents one section of your story. The first sentence is the beginning. The second sentence is the middle. And the third sentence is the end of the story. The elements that go into the beginning of a story will go into your first sentence. The elements that belong in the middle of a story will go into your second sentence. And the third sentence will contain the elements that belong at the end of a story.

The beginning is meant to tell the audience what they need to know for the rest of the story to make sense. This is known as the setup and in a memoir, or a family history story, it will probably contain mostly raw data. Family pictures may have this raw data written on the back of the image. If not, you may have to ask members of the family to tell you what they know about the picture. In either case, the information you have about the picture will form the beginning of your story. For example:

> *Around 1820, William Lindsey immigrated to America with his wife Nancy Crawford.*

Scrapbooks that don't use the Three-Sentence method often have something like this written about each picture. Facts about the picture are important to a story, but they are not a story by themselves. The facts establish the context which allows the reader to better understand what happens next. If you've already written a fact-filled sentence about a picture you can use that for the beginning of your story.

What the first sentence needs, in a Three-Sentence Story, are the elements that the writing industry calls "Setting." This includes:

1) When

2) Where

3) Who

4) What

5) Why

Don't panic. Putting all of this information into a single sentence is easy.

When did the story take place? This will be a date. It can be an exact date if that information is important, otherwise, just list the year. See I told you it'd be easy.

Where did the story take place? Just list the location. That can be any combination of town, state, and country or it could be a more generic location like, "the kitchen at Mom's house." Telling your audience, the location allows them to form a picture in their head and fill it with details. If the story doesn't include a picture, then readers can imagine how the people are dressed and what the buildings look like based on the location. And if there is a picture, they can include the sounds, smells, and other senses common there.

Who is the story about and who else is in the story? A name, or names, are all you need to tell the reader who the story is about. It can be the person's proper name. It can include their relationship to you, and it can also include nicknames.

Because the beginning is only one sentence long, the What and Why of the story can either be combined or one of the two left out. Including too much information increases the chance of making the first sentence hard to read and may even require too much guesswork on your part.

What did the people in the story do? This can be a brief description of the situation the person is in. Or it can be a goal the person has. Either one provides the reason why the action that takes place in the middle of the story was necessary.

Why did the people in the story do what they did? Explaining why a person does something allows the audience to feel as if they know that individual better. This is called "Characterization," in the writing industry, and is used to make audiences more sympathetic towards the characters in the story.

Let's see how all of these elements fit into a single sentence:

Around 1820. William Lindsey and his wife, Nancy Crawford, immigrated to America in order to escape religious prejudice in Ireland.

When does the story take place? Around 1820. Even though I don't have any pictures of William and Nancy, my audience can imagine what that time period might look like.

Where does the story take place? It starts in Ireland and ends in the United States. Most of the audience will have an idea what both places look like and should be able to picture them in their heads.

Who is the story about? It's about William Lindsey and wife, Nancy Crawford. I could have added that they're my great-great-great-grandparents, but that lengthens the sentence more than I desire. I could have also just identified them as my g-g-g-grandparents. Or I could refer to William as William "The Immigrant" Lindsey. That's not really his nickname, but it's what I call him.

What did the people in the story do and why did they do it? William and Nancy immigrated to America and they did it to escape the religious prejudice that was common in Ireland during that time.

That was easy.

The second sentence/middle of your story is where the action takes place. This is where most of the struggles happen in a traditional story. In a Three-Sentence Story, all of your action and struggles take place in a single sentence.

Don't worry. This is easier than it sounds.

Struggles happen when people have different goals and don't agree about what they should do. Like a disagreement my parents had over which Thanksgiving traditions they would keep from each of their families. Turkey or duck? Squash or yams? Pumpkin pie or pecan pie?

Obviously, the blending of holiday traditions wasn't a big, horrible dispute that ruined the lives of many people. It was a tiny, tiny conflict. And that's alright, because this is a tiny, tiny story. Struggles in a Three-Sentence Story can be something with serious consequences or they can be something minor.

Think of action and struggles as a description for the kind of sentence you want to use in the middle of your story. An action sentence might tell about a family who struggled to cross the plains on their journey west. Or it might discuss some of the challenges of running a farm during a major drought. Struggle sentences are more about people having opposing goals or opposite views on a topic, such as, a feud between two families in the bakery business. Or a disagreement your parents had over which Thanksgiving traditions they would keep with their families.

For example:

> *The township of Meigs, where William settled, was on the American frontier and life there meant a new kind of struggle for the immigrants.*

The mention of frontier life and struggle both give a sense of action in this sentence, which could be made even more dramatic by changing how the words are used. If I stated William struggled to survive on the American frontier, it would certainly sound more intense, but I don't actually know if that's true.

Disagreements are not the only form of conflict in stories, there's also competition between rivals. A story might tell a feud between two families in the bakery business or how a person competed against another athlete for the quarterback position on the high school football team. A competition sentence might go like this:

> *Mr. Jones opened a bakery in downtown Knoxville and had to continually improve his best recipes just to keep from losing customers to the Crompton Bakery across the street.*

Challenges are another form of struggle. This represents problems caused by nature, or a tough situation. It could be a story about the difficulty of running a farm during a major drought. A challenge sentence might go like this:

> *A severe drought hit the region and John had to take a job in town just to feed his family because the farm wasn't producing enough food.*

Obstacles to a stated goal is one of the easiest struggles to write about. All you need is a goal and then to list one or more obstacles that stood in the way of reaching the goal. For example:

> *Sarah worked summers at the resort to save enough money for college, but then had to use her savings to pay for her mother's medical bills.*

Mysteries and facing the unknown—What's in the box? Who's at the door? Will there be any farmland available when the pioneers reach their destination? Any sentence that leaves the audience wondering what will happen, or wanting to know more, provides this sort of mental struggle. For example:

> *John and Sarah purchased land in Missouri that the locals considered haunted.*

The great thing about this last example is that it doesn't matter if the land was haunted, or not, the suggestion alone is enough to grab the reader's interest.

Finally, you have the third sentence. This is the end of the story, but it can be helpful to look at it another way. To quote the *Goosebumps* movie, "Every story ever told can be divided into three distinctive parts: the beginning, the middle, and **the twist**."[2] You want to end your Three-Sentence Story with something that will make the audience marvel. Surprise them. Delight them. Add that extra element to make the story memorable.

Here's the third sentence for my story:

> *It appears that William was the only member of his family to make the move to Ohio, the location for the rest of the Lindsey's is unknown.*

The twist in this story is the revelation that William is the only Lindsey from Ireland that anything is known about. A twist doesn't have to be a major, mind-blowing surprise. It just has to be interesting. Afterall, this is a tiny, tiny story.

What makes the third sentence so easy to write is that you already know what happens. This is something from the past. You have the advantage of being able to look at everything that happened to the person in the story and then pick out the details that no one expected.

Didn't I mention that this would be Easy-Peasy?

Here's my Three-Sentence Story that I used as an example. When you read all three sentences together, it sounds like a story:

2 *Goosebumps*. Dir. Rob Letterman. Columbia Pictures, 2015. Film.

Around 1820. William Lindsey and his wife, Nancy Crawford, immigrated to America in order to escape the religious prejudice in Ireland. The township of Meigs was on the American frontier and life there represented a different kind of struggle for the Irish immigrants. It appears that William was the only member of his family to make the move to Ohio, the location for the rest of the Lindseys is unknown.

While my example uses three sentences to tell a story, don't feel limited to that number. The Three-Sentence Story is a suggestion to make it easier to write a super-tiny story about your picture. Your story could be two, or four, or however many sentences you want to use to tell what's important about the picture.

When deciding what to write in your mini story, try to include bits that tell us about the people. Bring them to life for the reader. Here is an example I borrowed from the book *John A. Whetten*, edited by Thomas F. Peterson:

"Mae Hamblin tells of a story that occurred at the mail station. 'One day, a renegade Indian was brought through, chained to the bottom of a wagon. John saw this and told his mother, who fixed a big plate of food and took it out. She demanded that the guards unchain the Indian's hands so he could eat. John watched the man eat. He didn't use a spoon but ate it all with his hands."

What makes this example interesting are the actions of the people in the story. In just a few sentences we can see what kind of person John's mother was, imagine what must have been going through John's mind, and reflect on the prisoner eating with his hands. It's the personal elements that make the story and the picture interesting.

No matter what size story you're writing, details are important. This topic will be covered in more depth later in this book, but here is an example:

William's children, Robert and James, gleefully riding Grandpa Crawford's horse on the ranch next to the Ohio River mill.

This final example shows the importance of personal details. The boys in the picture aren't just riding a horse, they're riding Grandpa Crawford's horse. It would be even better if we knew the horse's name. In many cases, you may not know all the details about a picture, it's okay, just use what details you have and add a personal observation. In other words, what thoughts go through your head when you look at the picture?

Once you have a feel for how the Three-Sentence Story works, it won't be difficult to write longer stories. What's my beginning? What's my middle? What's my end? Boom, boom, boom. Then you can turn your Three-Sentence Story into a three-paragraph story, or a three-page story, or a three-chapter story. The same concepts that I described here are used to create stories of any size, it's just a matter of adding more details and more memories.

STATS ON THE SIDE

You don't have to get rid of important statistics altogether. Some facts can be included in the first sentence of a picture's Three-Sentence Story. Any other information you want your readers to know can be placed in a sidebar, which is a section of the book that runs along the edge of the page. Keep the amount of information in the sidebar to a minimum. Once a sidebar takes up more space on the page than the pictures and stories then it is no longer a sidebar. It has become the main part of the book.

The great thing about a sidebar is your audience will know the information is there, but they don't have to pay any attention to it if they aren't interested. This method allows family history researchers and fact fans to easily find the information and everyone else can ignore it.

Three-Sentence Story

William Lindsey settled in Ohio around 1822, occupying the plot of land next to his father-in-law and near several of Nancy's siblings.

The township of Sprigg was on the American frontier and life there represented a different kind of struggle fo the Irish immigrants.

It appears that William was the only memember of his family to make the move to Ohio, the location for the rest of the Lindsey's is unkinown.

A barn in Sprigg Township, Ohio

William Lindsey, his wife, Nancy Crawford, and their daugther, Cora, about 1890.

ANTHOLOGIES

A collection of short stories allows you to write your book one event at a time. The same is true about writing chapters for a longer book, like a family chronicle, but short stories feel easier. They don't have the same need to move from event to event as smoothly. If the idea of writing a series of short stories seems daunting to you, then have several members of the family write about the same person or event. Another advantage of an anthology is that it will allow you to gather short stories based on a theme rather than a plotline. Easy-peasy.

The disadvantage of writing an anthology is it requires quite a few events to write about. And if the theme isn't strong enough, the book can feel jumbled and confusing to the reader. However, both of these are minor disadvantages.

Collecting stories from family members represents a greater challenge. In addition to the effort it will take to convince people to write a story and then encourage them to finish the project, you will also have the duty of coordinating the process and editing the anthology. Despite the increased challenge, this kind of project can be extra fulfilling as you share and discuss stories with other family members. Think of these sessions as mini family reunions.

More Than Words

Just as a scrapbook doesn't have to be all pictures, an anthology doesn't have to be all words. Depending on the theme of the book, an anthology can benefit from including other elements. Pictures, images of letters or historical documents, or anything else that comes to mind will visually enhance your story.

You might also want to consider adding written elements that have a different format than your short stories. Recipes, jokes, and quotes all fit into this category and will stand out from the short story they accompany.

Any elements you add to a short story should match the tone of your theme. Recipes are a good match for an anthology about family holidays. Quotes taken from the person in the story make an excellent choice for an anthology about the life of your grandparents.

GRANNY'S CINNAMON ROLLS

A RECIPE BY JUDY BACKUS

INGREDIENTS

- 2 cups milk
- 2/3 cup butter, softened
- 1 teaspoon salt
- 1/2 cup sugar
- 2 T. yeast
- warm water
- 1 t. sugar

- flour
- 2 eggs
- butter
- sugar
- cinnamon or brown sugar

DIRECTIONS

- Scald milk, butter, salt, sugar.Let cool 'til warm.
- Put yeast in warm water with sugar & let dissolve. When yeast starts to bubble, add to milk mixture and start adding flour, 1/2 c. at a time. Stir good
- Add eggs.Keep adding flour until you have a thick batter & let rise
- When it comes to top of the bowl, add a little flour to mix until batter becomes a soft dough, let rise again; butter top of it.
- Then roll out, spread with butter & sprinkle wi/ sugar an cinnamon
- Bake 25 minutes at 350

Start with a Picture

Although it was mentioned above, the idea of placing a picture at the start of each short story in an anthology is worth repeating. A picture of a person or place in the story will help the audience keep that image in mind as they read about the events that take place. It may also help you to stay focused on what the story is about. And placing a picture in front of the short story helps with the formatting of the book. Picture. Short story. Picture. Short story. Easy-Peasy.

SHORT STORY TIPS

The same ideas that you learned from the Three-Sentence Story apply to short stories. They have a beginning, a middle, and an end. But you have room to write more about each section.

The Beginning - tells the reader when and where the story takes place, who is part of the story, and some sort of problem, question, or struggle they face.

Finding the struggle in a family history story is easy. First, the events have already taken place and second, you already know what happened and what those struggles were. Just figure out who was involved and what made it inevitable that there was going to be a problem, then describe the situation to the reader.

Keep in mind struggles happen because the person has a goal, or desire, and then obstacles get in the way. How a person overcomes those obstacles is the reason people like stories. Make sure to include what influences made the person in your story pick that goal.

The Middle – is all about complications. What obstacles develop to make it more difficult for the person in the story to achieve their goal? What do they struggle with to solve a problem, receive an answer, or obtain something they want? Think about what things made the situation worse and what things made the situation better too. There's no reason to leave out the good stuff.

Who else was involved in the story? How did they react to the events? Did they have the same goals as the person you're writing about? Or did they want a different outcome for the situation? Who helped and what did they do to help? Who got in the way or actually tried to prevent the person in your story from succeeding? All of these elements add to the excitement of a good story.

The End should have a resolution to the problem, question, or struggle mentioned at the beginning of the story. This doesn't have to be a happy ending because these are part of a larger life story, the short stories can end in failure. For example, you might be writing about an ancestor who wanted to marry a woman, but was turned down and that led to him meeting the woman he actually married. The end of the one story is sad, until the reader finds out in a later story that it created an opportunity to marry someone else.

If possible, you want to include some sort of twist at the end of the story. What is it about the situation which ended in an unexpected way? Was there some benefit or unforeseen consequence involved in the resolution? Or maybe someone reacted to the final turn of events in a way that no one expected? If there is something that surprised or delighted you, then your reader will probably have the same reaction.

The great thing about including twists in your family stories is that you already know what things happened that were amazing. You know which events happened that nobody foresaw. Write stories about those events. If the person you're writing about says, "If only I'd known," then write that story, because the reader isn't going to see it coming either.

Here's a couple more tips for writing short stories:

Focus on one event or problem – a short story about how a farming family struggled during a drought doesn't need to include how the oldest daughter wanted to attend college. Unless the drought had an impact on that situation.

Things need to change – write about what's different for the person than from when the story started. And write about how those changes make the person in the story feel. Maybe you have a family member who wanted to leave the family business, but ended up working a different job in the same industry. That works if the message of your story is the things the person learned as a child were a constant part of his adult life. Or that he couldn't escape the early influences in his life.

SAMPLE TEMPLATE

Not everyone is good at thinking up themes for scrapbooks and anthologies. No problem. Templates provide a list of events that fit together to form a larger story. Select an appropriate story for each event and when you are done writing, you will have an anthology that covers the generic parts of a person's life.

Chapter 1 – Birth. This short story can be about how the parents met, any unusual events associated with the person's birth, or even about the place where they were born.

Chapter 2 – Childhood. Pick a story, or two, about the person's life as a child. Who were their friends, what did they like to do, did any major events happen during their youth? How did their childhood shape their future?

Chapter 3 – School. Where did the person go to school and what was it like? Did they make any lifelong friends? Did the person develop a lifelong love for a particular study or activity?

Chapter 4 – Dating and marriage. Is there an interesting story about dating? Did the person date someone who eventually became famous? Or did the person marry their high school sweetheart? Pick a story that stands out and tell it. Add a second chapter if you want to tell about the wedding day.

Chapter 5 – Professional Life #1. What jobs did this person have early in their adult life? Describe the first career they chose to work in. List any big events that took place.

Chapter 6 – Family #1. Tell a story about being newlyweds. Or about early family life. This can be multiple chapters if you want to discuss each of the children that are born to a couple.

Chapter 7 – Important Event #1. Decide what's the most important thing to happen to that person and then write a story about it. Did this person nearly die? Did they invent the internet? This should be a big, life-changing event.

Chapter 8 – Professional Life #2. Tell a story about the person's career, later in life. Did they stay in the same industry or change to a different one? What professional accomplishments did that person achieve?

Chapter 9 – Family #2. Is there an interesting story about the family when the children are older, or even once they've all left the nest? Did the family take any memorable vacations?

Chapter 10 – Important Event #2. What other events took place that affected the person, or even the family as a whole? This can include the death of parents, grandparents, and other family members.

> *And this doesn't have to be limited to a single chapter, write multiple chapters that involve important events if they exist.*

> *Chapter 11 – Wrap It Up. Is there a story that expresses your final thoughts on whatever message you want to share with your audience? Perhaps a last reflection of what they learned from living with someone who faced a serious health challenge, a disability or even the death of a spouse.*

A template is merely a tool to help you think of which stories work together to form a complete book, to create a larger story. The chapter topics are just suggestions. Change them around. If you want six chapters in row about the birth of each child in a family . . . then write six straight chapters about children being born. You don't even have to write about the children's births. You can pick a story from their youth that perfectly describes them.

None of our lives follow a perfect pattern. An important, life-changing event can happen at any point in our lives. Move the Important Event story to where it fits in the template. Rearrange the chapters in a way that best represents the life of the person you are writing about.

NOTES

NOTES

INTERVIEW YOUR WAY
TO A STORY

Interviews are one of the most powerful tools available to a storyteller. The right questions will allow you to find a story, develop that story, and then fill the story with the sort of details that will bring it to life. All you need is a person to interview and a way to record their answers.

Alright, maybe that's not all. You also need a list of questions to ask. And if you ask the right questions, the story almost writes itself. The trick to interviewing your way to a successful story is knowing which questions to ask and how to ask them.

The Easy-Peasy Method has you covered. This chapter includes guidelines on how to interview a person and a large list of questions. The questions have been separated into categories to make it easy to discover the right kind of information for any stage of your story. More about that later—here's how to prepare yourself for a successful interview.

GUIDELINES FOR A SUCCESSFUL INTERVIEW

Interview Guideline # 1 – Ask open-ended questions.

Avoid questions that can be answered with a simple yes, or no. Instead, ask questions that give the person you are interviewing plenty of ways to answer. You want questions that invite the person being interviewed to tell a story about their life. Sometimes, you're still going to get one-word answers. When that happens, follow up by asking them, "Why?" or, "How did that make you feel?" And remember the very effective, "What happened next?" Asking leading questions should give you a longer and more interesting answer.

Interview Guideline # 2 – Ask one question at a time.

Even if an answer brings more questions to mind, wait until the person is finished with their answer before moving on to the next one. By cutting them off early, you distract the person and risk losing some fascinating elements to their story.

Interview Guideline # 3 – Be patient.

Give the person you're interviewing enough time to answer the questions. Sometimes, it takes a few moments to pull details from memory. Rushing a person through an interview can result in key moments of their life being left behind. Let the person tell the story at their own pace. If the person is having difficulty remembering details, try asking different questions about the same event. Try looking at the story using a different perspective, like, "How did this event make you feel?" For more details, ask, "Do you remember any sounds, smells, or tastes that were part of the event?" These kinds of questions may trigger memories the person may not have remembered otherwise.

Interview Guideline # 4 – Look for the hook.

If part of the person's answer grabs your attention, ask for more details. Ask as many questions as you need in order to tell the full story. Chances are that if you find whatever was said to be interesting, then so will others.

Interview Guideline # 5 – Look for what's inside.

The truly great interview questions reveal what a person thinks of themselves. These are questions that not only show the true nature of a person but lead to memorable stories.

Interview Guideline # 6 – Respect the privacy of others.

Some questions may be too personal, or painful, for the person you are interviewing to answer. Move on. There will be plenty of other interesting and personal moments to write about. Whatever story might be had, by pursuing an uncomfortable or painful topic, is not worth hurting the person to get it.

QUESTION CATEGORIES

Interviews will allow you to discover exciting details about a living person. The questions can also be used to find information about a deceased person from those who knew them. You can also answer the questions yourself to develop story ideas for a memoir.

Each of the categories below focuses on a different aspect of a person's life. If you want to write about your parent's courtship and marriage, ask a few questions from the Dating and Marriage category. If you want to write a memoir that reveals the inner you, ask yourself questions from the Insightful category and see what story develops from your answers.

Questions have been placed into all appropriate categories. That means you may see the same question in more than one category.

Here are the categories and suggestions on how to use them.

Youth – This category covers events and memories from childhood through high school graduation. If part of your story takes place during the person's youth, then this category will give you details from that time period. It is useful in showing where a person started out and the early influences on their life. Questions from this category work best when you compare the answers to events taken from later in the person's life. Keep in mind that entertaining stories are all about change and this can be a good place to start.

School –This can include elementary school, high school, or college. It represents life outside the home, during our informative years. This is a great category for discovering the people who had a major influence in the life of the person you are writing about, and includes, family, teachers, coaches or other mentors.

The school years also have a tremendous impact on the career a person selects. If you want to fully explore the professional life of a person, this is a good place to start the journey.

Dating and Marriage – The choice of who we marry is probably the most important decision we will ever make. It is the blending of two families who may be very different from one another. It can be a source of major struggle in a person's life, but, more importantly, this is where we go to add romance to our stories. Romance is good. *Don't tell my wife I said that.*

A story about an entire family can start with the courtship of the parents. Even if you decide the story doesn't start there, a few questions from this category should probably be included somewhere along the way.

Family Life – This category covers family relationships—Parents and children, siblings, grandparents and grandchildren, aunts, uncles, and cousins. The questions in this category can be applied to any time period. This is an essential category if you are writing family stories and want to give future generations a picture of what life was like for the family you're writing about.

Family History – These questions are intended to add life to the dry details of traditional family histories. The lives of family members who have passed away are more than dates of their birth, marriage, and death and locations on a map. These people worked, had interesting events happen to them, and left behind a legacy of some sort. Finding the answers to these questions should help you turn the facts into an actual story.

Holidays – Family traditions are an important part of most holidays. In a way, they define families. This category can be used to create a theme for your story or to create moments that will bond the reader to the family they are reading about. Just thinking about Christmas celebrations can brighten the mood for many readers.

Personal Life – The answers to these questions will tell you what a person is like. Learn their likes and dislikes, what made them happy or sad and how they reacted to situations. Answers and information to such questions will bring the person, you are writing about, to life to individuals who have never met them.

Professional Life – The job a person has affects all the other parts of their life. In some cases, a person's career might be the actual story you want to tell. This category is also an excellent source of conflict. Although you may not want conflict in your life, it's a good thing in stories. A person's career life and their home life often pull the individual in opposite directions, and that makes for a story that will interest your readers.

Hometown – All stories take place somewhere. In many cases, the place where a person or family lives is part of the story. At the very least, the hometown provides a visual element that can place readers into the setting. The hometown can be at the center of your story, providing a theme from which to pull the stories of several people together.

Friends – In a sense, friends are the family we pick for ourselves. Who a person chooses to spend their time with and what they do together tells us much about that individual. If the person you are interviewing has a friend who is a celebrity, or a person of note, then the story might be about their relationship. This category can also be used to provide some fun elements to your story in between the serious moments.

Important Events – This list covers the significant events of a person's life. They can be strung together as a template to tell a life story, or they can be used to discover the story you want to tell about that person. You may even find there are several stories worth telling and once you know which story you want to tell; these questions can help fill out the important elements of that story.

Crossroads – These questions are perfect, for finding a theme for your story because they usually represent a turning-point in a person's life. Select additional categories that will show life before the crossroad event and life after the crossroad event. It's best to use only one crossroad event in a story, unless they somehow relate to one another.

Personal Views – This is a great category for getting acquainted with the person in the story. What were their likes and dislikes, and how did they feel about events in the story? What motivates them, in the writing industry, this is what is known as characterization. Audiences root for people who they understand and want to read more about them. Show your readers what the person in your story is thinking and why they think that way and you will have the audience wanting to find out what happens next.

Insights - These are meant to be thought-provoking questions. Just like the Important Events category, they can be used to discover the story you want to tell. Best of all, these questions can result in some of the most interesting bits to use in the story. And they will provide you with items that feel meaningful to the reader.

INTERVIEW TO FIND A STORY

One of the hardest parts of writing a story is deciding what you want to write about. It doesn't matter if you're writing about your great-aunt Nancy or your personal memoir, each of our lives are filled with dozens of compelling stories. Interviews are a great way to discover the story you want to write. The only difference is whether you're going to ask yourself these questions or ask someone else.

To show you how this works, let's put together a story about my grandmother.

First, I look through the Important Events and Insightful categories for questions that can help me develop a theme for the story. In everyday terms, that means I want to select an idea that will be at the heart of my story, so that I can build a series of events (mini-stories) around it.

There are a lot of great choices here and I might have to ask the person a few questions until they give a compelling answer which I feel will make a great story. The Important Events category offers me the following questions that interest me:

- What is the best thing that ever happened to you?

- What is the worst thing that ever happened to you?

- Have you experienced any natural disasters?

It turns out that my grandmother did not have a natural disaster story. Finding out the best thing that ever happened to her would probably make a good story, but I'm convinced that seeing how she grew from a bad experience and what she learned along the way is a better story.

Then I look at the Insight category. I like the following questions from the list:

- Ø Tell me your favorite story about yourself or someone you know.

- Ø What is the one thing you want the world to remember about you?

- Ø What is the hardest choice you ever had to make?

Having a person tell their favorite story gives insight into who they are. Not only do you have the story itself to work with, but the answer should also give you an idea of why the story is important to the person. This reveals personality and allows you to write the story so that it better reflects the person's point of view. The other two questions do much of the same thing. They give a basic story and insight as to why that event in the person's life was important to them.

For example, I decide to write a story about the worst thing that happened to my grandmother and try to include a section where I tell her favorite story. The worst thing that happened to my grandmother is that she and my grandfather lost all of their money and had to move across the country. Her favorite story is about her father's journey from simple farmer to owning a series of farms and the first car dealership in the area where they lived.

Now, I have a story idea. It starts when my grandmother is just a girl and continues past the time that her and my grandfather lose the money they inherited. Maybe I add a few chapters on how those events affected their children, which includes my father.

INTERVIEW TO DEVELOP A STORY

Once you know which story it is you want to tell, you can use the interview questions to bring out all the details needed to make the events interesting. Keep the main focus of the story in mind as you look through the questions. Pick the ones that will make that story meaningful. Questions about how it started. Questions about who was involved. Questions about how it ended. And questions about how the people involved reacted to the events in the story.

Using the example of my grandmother's story, I decide to pick a few questions about when she was a child. This is where her story starts and it will give me a chance to see what her life was like before she lost the money. Here are the questions from the Youth category that I want to use for the story.

- Tell me about your childhood home.

- Tell me about your parents.

- What is your favorite holiday memory as a child?

- Describe a typical family meal.

- What did your father do for a living?

Then I might include a couple of questions from the School category, especially from high school and college. The answers to those questions will give me an idea of what it was like for my grandmother as she grew into an adult.

The Dating and Marriage category will give me events I can use in my story that involve both of my grandparents as they lived on their own. Family Life, Professional Life, and Hometown can give me plenty of material for the events that led up to my grandparents losing all of their money. Then I can finish with a couple of questions from Personal Views. Questions that focus specifically on the topic of how they lost their money and how they felt about it.

Boom! I have a story about my grandmother's life.

Easy-Peasy.

INTERVIEW TO CREATE A THEME

Memoirs and family stories are not meant to tell *all* of the events in a person's life. A story that started when a person was born and continued until they died would be thousands of pages long. Not only that, but an event-by-event story about a person's life would be dull. Instead, you want a theme. All of the events you include in a story should relate to that theme. By using a theme, the story, or stories, if it is an anthology, come together in a way that makes sense to the reader.

When deciding on a theme, you want to use a single question. A single idea that is then expanded to create an entire story. If you happen to be crazy about Christmas, write a story that moves from your holiday memories as a child, through your teen years, your first Christmas as a married couple, with your children, and then perhaps end with an especially meaningful Christmas involving the grandchildren and extended family. How about a childhood tour of the holidays as a way to preserve the traditions you remember as a child? Or the story could be a collection of your visits with Grandma and what you learned from her.

First, pick a question for your theme. Then, interview as many people as necessary to develop the idea. And finally, choose additional questions to fill in the details for your story.

For example, in the Dating and Marriage category, one of the questions asks, "What is your spouse's greatest talent?" From that question, I decide I want to write a story about the spouses who married into my family. Interviews will need to be done with myself and my siblings. I look through the questions in other categories to help me fill in the details of the story. In addition to the theme question, I choose the following:

From the School category, "What was important to you as a teenager?" This question might help me to show where and how the spouses gained their talent. At the very least it gives me the attributes that led to where the spouse's talents are now.

From the Personal Life category, "What accomplishment are you most proud about?" There's a chance that the spouses are proud of the same talents that have been noticed by you and your siblings. If not, the question can give you a trait to compare, or contrast, to the one you are writing about.

From the Professional category, "If you could have any job, what would it be?" How would the spouses' talent impact the way they do their dream job? How does it impact the way they perform in their current job? Is there any connection between their talent and the job they wish they had?

Then I could wrap it up with a question like, "What is the best moment you've had that involves to your talent?" Or ask, "How do you think having that talent has changed your life?" I just made up those last two questions and you should feel free to create questions of your own, too. The point of these questions is to find an event, or thought, that allows you to end the story with an important insight about the spouse.

INTERVIEW FOR MEMOIR

Interviewing for a memoir is the same as interviewing for any other story. The only difference is you will be asking yourself these questions.

If you're writing a memoir that's meant to be a history of your life, you can move through the categories in a chronological matter i.e., Youth, School, Dating and Marriage, Professional Life, and Family Life. However, without a theme, it's likely to be dull. Even if you're writing for future generations, you want your story to be interesting. Consider picking questions from each of these categories that apply to a central idea.

The Important Events, Crossroads, and Insight categories are best for picking memoir themes. They tend to represent major problems a person confronts in life. The questions in these categories also address concerns other people have, making the story feel familiar to the reader. Memoirs usually cover only the events that are related to the theme. If your Crossroad event is the discovery that your dad is not your biological father, then write about those things related to that theme.

Based on the Crossroad event above, I wrote a memoir about how the discovery of a different biological father affected my life. From the Youth category, I wrote about my oldest memory, which happened to include my other dad, who raised me. Instead of using the most embarrassing moment as a child, I used one of the most terrifying moments. (Notice how I changed the question to better suit my purpose?) And I also made use of the question about any injuries as a child, even though what I wrote about wasn't a major injury.

Those events all had a connection to the man who raised me and showed the kind of relationship we had. They described, to my readers, what my normal life was like. At least, the parts of my life that fit into the theme of my story.

A Crossroad event might only represent a couple of years of your life. Not everything that happened to you during that time—just the events related to your theme. My memoir covers a two-year period and has several points where it skips ahead several months. I only included moments that were significant to the discovery that I had a different biological father than my siblings.

For example, here is the outline I developed for *The Milkman's Son*. A story that uncovers my discovery of the man who I thought was my dad was not actually my biological father.

After I decided this was an event I wanted to write about, I determined a time frame for the story. The majority of *The Milkman's Son* takes place during a two-year period. I spent a few chapters leading up to the decision to take a DNA test, but the real story starts there and ends with my return from a second visit to my New Jersey family. That space of time is when all of the shock and emotion of the event impacted me. All of the changes to my life from this discovery happened during the time.

Then I decided on a theme and picked out ideas and events that were important to the message I wanted to share with everyone. The message, or theme, of my story is, "Blood doesn't define family. It is the love we share that makes us family," because, that's what I learned from my experience. I wanted to quiet people's fear of meeting family for the first time. I wanted to encourage people to take DNA tests and find out the truth.

These are the ideas that I used to create my outline.

1. A visit with my dad where he discussed family ghosts visiting him in his dreams and then asked me to do our family history.

2. Discoveries about the family tree and how much fun it was to research.

3. Hitting a research wall and the decision to take a DNA test.

4. What the DNA testing process was like.

5. The emotion of discovering that my dad was not my biological father.

6. The fear and hesitation that nearly prevented me from meeting my new family.

7. The reaction of members of both families, in Arizona and in New Jersey.

8. What it was like to get to know my new family. What they were like.

9. My trip to New Jersey to visit my new family.

10. The aftermath of my visit. (Not everyone was happy with how well I got along with the new family members and my desire to be closer to them.)

11. What it meant to me when my new-found father was hospitalized.

12. How my mother helped me to make a second trip to see my father.

13. Stories I heard from family members in New Jersey who had a similar situation to me.

14. A discussion of what it was like to adopt two children, because I wanted to look at what makes a family a family and these adopted boys are family.

15. Final thoughts on what all of it meant.

From there, I picked out specific events that would help me show the points I wanted to make. For instance, the title of my memoir comes from my siblings in Arizona. They have called me the milkman's son for years, noticing that I do not look like any of them, not at all. Then I added scenes from when they laughed at my DNA results. They found it humorous because it was proof that I was, indeed, the milkman's son. I included a few scenes where I mentioned it to my wife, my children, my friends, and acquaintances. All of these gave me different perspectives and reactions to use in exploring my situation.

Then, once I had all the events picked out, I started writing the story. I inserted details to make each event seem real in the reader's minds and included enough emotion so they could feel the events as they happened to me.

That's it. One crossroad event that resulted in an entire book.

INTERVIEW FOR ANTHOLOGIES

An anthology is a collection of short stories. This sort of book works best if all the stories are connected by a theme. A family anthology might be about how everyone reacted to the news of grandma's death and how they dealt with her loss.

All of the short stories should use the same theme and answer the same questions. If the anthology is a memoir, then the same questions would be asked, but they would apply to different times in your life. By using the same questions, you tie all of the short stories together into one larger story.

As an example, use the following interview question from the Family category. "Tell me about your favorite day with your family." Change that to, "Tell me about your favorite day with Granny."

Write a short story about your favorite day with Granny—as a Youth. Then write about your favorite day with Granny while you were in high school or dating your wife. Check the categories and continue to write stories about your favorite day with Granny through the lens of Family Life, Holiday, Family History, Hometown, Friends, and Personal Life.

INTERVIEW FOR FAMILY CHRONICLES

Family chronicles usually cover events that take place over years of time. These stories are best if they show how the people involved have changed. They have a beginning, middle, and end that all look at the theme from different points in time. Pick questions to demonstrate how the people and situations change.

The difference between an anthology and a family chronicle is that the events in an anthology are complete stories on their own. Whereas the events in a family chronicle tend to flow as one, long, continuous story. Otherwise, you can use the same methods as described in the anthology section above.

ADAPTABLE QUESTIONS

My free, downloadable pamphlet, *How to Interview Your Way to a Story* has over a hundred questions. That sounds like a lot, but it isn't enough to cover every possible situation. If you find that you're not getting the right answers for the story you want to tell, then mix-up the questions. Take a question from the Dating and Marriage category and find a way to make it about the person's professional life. Substitute a key word in a question for another that works better for your purposes. If the question asks about Christmas, but you want to write about Valentine's Day, then make that change.

The interview questions are meant to be a tool to help you discover the story you want to tell. Make them work for you – not the other way around.

* The list of questions in this book are meant as a starting point for your interviews. Use the link below for access to more questions on the downloadable version of *How to Interview Your Way to a Story.*

www.easypeasymethod.com/memoir-resources

QUESTION LIST

YOUTH

Where were you born? How did your family end up there?

What's your oldest memory?

Tell me about your childhood home.

Tell me about your parents.

Tell me a story about your siblings.

Who was your best childhood friend? What were they like?

Tell me about any childhood pets.

Describe a typical family meal.

What was your favorite thing to do as a child?

Did you have any major diseases or injuries as a child? Tell me about them.

What did you want to grow up to be as an adult?

SCHOOL

What was your favorite subject in school?

What is your favorite memory about school?

What was your least favorite part of the school day?

Describe yourself as a student.

Tell me about the friends you had in school.

What did you plan to do as an adult, either career or personal goal?

What was your most embarrassing moment in school?

What was important to you as a teenager?

Tell me about your teenage social life.

Who most influenced you in school i.e., teacher, friend, another student?

Describe a typical day during high school.

DATING AND MARRIAGE

Tell me about the first date with your spouse.

Tell me about the best moment you had with your spouse.

How did you meet your spouse?

What memory stands out about your wedding day?

What do you admire most about your spouse?

What do you believe is the key to a successful marriage?

What goals did you and your spouse make together?

What was your most embarrassing moment while you were dating? And married?

What annoys you most about your spouse?

What was a conflict you had to resolve? How did you resolve it?

Tell me about the first time you met your in-laws.

FAMILY LIFE

How did your parents meet?

Tell me about the day your first child was born.

What is special about your home?

What is your favorite family activity?

Tell me about your favorite day with your family.

What is the most important advice your parents gave you?

What was the most difficult thing about raising children?

Tell me the story of how you picked your children's names.

What do you love and admire about your siblings? Your children?

Has your family experienced any natural disasters?

FAMILY HISTORY

Is there a naming tradition in your family?

What stories have been passed along about your parents, grandparents or other ancestors?

Do you have any famous, or infamous, relatives in your family tree?

What is your favorite story about close, or extended family members, or ancestors?

Have any family recipes been passed down to you?

Describe any physical traits that run in your family.

Are there any special family photos, heirlooms, or treasures that have been passed down?

Do you have any family customs that originated in a foreign land?

What did your father/grandfather do for a living?

Do you have a middle name? What does it represent?

HOLIDAYS

What is your favorite holiday? Why?

How did your family celebrate Christmas when you were a child?

What is your favorite Christmas tradition?

What is your favorite holiday activity?

What is your least favorite holiday? Why?

Who did you spend the holidays with?

What is your favorite holiday location as either an adult or a child?

What is your favorite holiday food?

Tell me an embarrassing holiday story.

What annoys you most about the holidays?

PERSONAL LIFE

Tell me a story that involves your favorite place.

What is your favorite thing to do?

Have you had any major diseases or injuries as an adult? Tell me about them.

What is the most amazing thing that has happened to you?

Tell me about your most embarrassing moment as an adult.

What is your greatest pet peeve?

Tell me about a family member that you miss.

What is the funniest thing that has ever happened to you?

Tell me about the best day you ever had.

What is your favorite story that you've heard other people talk about you?

PROFESSIONAL LIFE

Tell me about your first job.

Tell me about your favorite job.

If you could have any job, what would it be? Why?

What is the worst job you ever had?

Who is your favorite person to work with?

Who is your least favorite person to work with?

Did you choose your career? How did you end up working in your profession?

What professional achievement are you most proud of? Why?

Do you have a nickname at work? What is the origin of that name?

What annoys you most about work?

HOMETOWN

Where were you born? How did your family end up there?

Tell me about your childhood home?

What other families lived in your childhood neighborhood?

What was your least favorite thing about your childhood neighborhood?

What is your least favorite thing about the city/town/neighborhood where you live now?

Tell me about a fad that was popular in your city/town/neighborhood.

Tell me about the worst event to happen in your hometown.

Tell me a favorite story about your childhood neighborhood.

Describe walking down the main street of your home town.

What is your home town's best feature, attraction, or industry?

FRIENDS

Who was your best childhood friend? What was they like?

Tell me about your favorite friend as an adult.

Did you have a lot of friends as a child, just a few, or only one?

What is your favorite thing to do with your friends?

Pick a friend and tell me what you admire most about that person.

Do your friends have a nickname for you? Why did they name you that?

Where is your favorite place to hang out with friends?

Tell me an embarrassing story involving your friends.

What annoys you the most about your friends?

Tell me about a friend that you miss.

IMPORTANT EVENTS

Where were you born? How did your family end up there?

Did you suffer any major injuries or contract any serious illnesses?

Tell me about your wedding day.

Were you ever mentioned in a newspaper?

What is the best thing that ever happened to you?

What is the worst thing that ever happened to you?

What world event had the biggest impact on you? Did it directly affect your family?

Which of your accomplishments means the most to you?

Tell me about something, or someone, that helped yu grow or change.

Have you experienced any natural disasters?

CROSSROADS

Tell me about a choice you made that effected your career.

Tell me about a choice you made that changed your life.

Tell me about a choice you made that you wish you could take back.

Tell me about an important choice you made while dating.

What is the hardest choice you ever had to make?

What is the most amazing thing that has happened to you?

Tell me about something, or someone, that helped you grow or change.

Tell me about buying your first home.

What's the worst trouble you ever got into?

Tell me about an event that changed your life.

PERSONAL VIEWS

What church did your family attend when you were a child?

What church did you attend as an adult?

What world event had the biggest impact on you? Did it directly affect your family?

Have you ever stood up for something you believe, even when it was hard to do? When?

What view or belief do you have that conflicts with most of the people you know?

How would you classify yourself?

What do you daydream about most?

What scares you? Why?

Share a principal you have learned or one that you have taught.

What are your most precious and deeply embedded values?

INSIGHTFUL

Tell me your favorite story about yourself or someone you know.

What is the one thing you want the world to remember about you?

What is the scariest thing you ever experienced?

What is the best thing that ever happened to you?

What is the worst thing that ever happened to you?

What haven't we talked about that you would like to discuss?

What is the biggest obstacle you had to overcome?

If you could change something about yourself, what would it be?

What is something few people know about you?

How is the world different from when you were a child?

NOTES

NOTES

CREATING A STORYLINE

How do you condense 40+ years of a person's life into a few hundred pages? You do that by only including the parts which help to tell the story you want to tell. Leave the rest out. The first step in that process is to find the specific story that you want everyone to know.

EVENT-FILLED LIVES

Stories are basically a series of events strung together in a way that makes sense to the readers. An event is something that happened.

Going to a job interview is an event. Thanksgiving dinner is an event for anyone who celebrates the holiday and even for some who don't. Getting married is an event.

Events in a story should have some connection to the message you want to tell people. If your message is to educate others about what a great marriage Grandma and Grandpa had, then you will want to include plenty of events that show different aspects of their married life.

An event includes people who are doing something, or want to do something. Obstacles or struggles can stand in the way or make it more difficult for people to do what they want. I mean, when was the last time Thanksgiving dinner went exactly as planned? During an event, people have thoughts and feelings about whatever is happening. An event eventually ends. It can end successfully or it can end in some sort of failure. And the people at the event will have more thoughts and feelings about the way the event ended.

All of the parts of an event are important to a story. For each one that's left out, the story is weakened. Here's a little checklist you can use as you write about each event.

- Decide on an event.

- Include anyone who was part of the event.

- Include what the people wanted to do.

- Insert any problems, struggles, or obstacles that made their plans more difficult to do.

- Include any thoughts and feelings the person in the story had about the event, the other people involved, and any challenges they faced during the event.

- Describe how the event ended, especially on how it did or did not meet expectations.

- Include any thoughts and feelings the person in the story had about how the event ended.

Repeat this process for each event in your story. Easy-peasy.

BEGINNINGS, MIDDLES, AND ENDS

If you're thinking this looks familiar . . . you're right. That's because it's an important concept for any story. The suggestions in this chapter work for stories of any length, from tiny, Three-Sentence Stories all the way up to full-length books.

Professional writers often work from formulas to determine the ideal length for each section of the story. But that's too complicated. Instead of worrying about keeping the beginning portion of the book to a specific number of pages or a certain percentage of the entire story, just write until you've included everything that needs to be there. Then write the middle the same way, and then, write the end. Easy-peasy.

DON'T START AT THE BEGINNING

It seems reasonable to start every story at the beginning, but this often results in the reader sifting through details. Details which don't have anything to do with the message you want them to know. This, in turn, may cause the reader to lose interest.

Instead of starting at the beginning of the story, jump into the middle of an unusual situation or when a problem is introduced. Readers are instinctively drawn to events that are out of the ordinary and to problems that arise. Humans want to know what's going to happen next. That sort of start is known as a hook.

For example: Rather than write about a family's decision to immigrate to America the story might be more exciting if it started as they boarded the ship to cross the ocean. Write about the dangers of the trip and the feelings the person in the story might have about leaving their home. If the trip included a life-threatening storm, all the better!

Anything that grabs a reader's attention is a hook. Here is a list of some of the different kinds of hooks you can use in a story:

- A Question – this is an easy hook to use. Choose an event that happens later in the story and then create a question that it will answer. This doesn't have to be an actual question. Although, having one of your characters ask, "What does grandpa keep in that trunk in the attic?" will certainly grab the reader's attention.

- For example: the story starts when a young woman receives an acceptance letter to the college she has wanted to attend since grade school, but then questions how she will pay for tuition and living expenses now that her dream has come true.

- A Mystery – anything that the person doesn't figure out until much later in the story is a mystery. All this hook needs are a couple of hints about the mystery and then follow up with an occasional mention, during the story, that the answer has not been found.

- For example: the story starts with a trunk in the attic that has an old military uniform and a picture of your grandfather wearing it. Your grandfather has his arm around another young man. Who is the other person and why hasn't grandfather ever talked about his time in the military?

- An Unusual Situation – look for something out of the ordinary that happened to the person you are writing about. The situation doesn't have to be a major event in the person's life. It can be an amusing anecdote or even an embarrassing moment. The advantage for having this kind of a hook is that it gives the reader an idea of what the person in the story is like and that makes it interesting. For example, the story starts with your father leading a mule train through the mountains at sixteen. How did a boy from Long Beach end up working as a cowboy and why?

- A Conflict – exists when two people disagree over what to do, or when they are after the same thing and only one of them can have it. This does not have to be a big, horrible disagreement for it to work as the hook, but it should relate to the theme of the story. This could be as simple as two people who want the last piece of pie or as serious as a life-and-death struggle.

- For example, the story starts with an argument over money. Your grandmother promises to pay her brother back. Your uncle is upset that she took the money in the first place. How will that situation end? For my dad's parents, this conflict is perfect for a story with a theme about what living an irresponsible life does to a family. It kicks off the story that represents the last of the good times and the beginning of lean years where both my grandparents and their children struggled to make ends meet.

- A Contradiction – is a type of mystery. It can be as simple as a person acting strangely, but telling everyone they're alright. This kind of hook can be used to introduce the story's theme or conflict right from the start. If you tell the reader about a goal the person has and then show how their actions, or circumstances, work against that goal, the audience will want to see how the contradiction is resolved.

- For example, the story starts when your brother drives home in a brand-new car. He doesn't have a job or money in the bank. He says he bought it, but how is that possible?

- A Pivotal Moment – this is an important moment in the person's life. Not the important moment you are writing about, but maybe one that leads up to it. This can be a moment where the person makes a decision that changes their life.

- For example, the story starts with the death of a child because of the potato famine in Ireland, which triggers the decision to move to America.

- The Dread Factor – all this hook requires is a dark moment in a person's life. Make the audience wonder how the person will deal with the situation. This kind of hook works best if the dark moment has something to do with the message you want to share with the audience.

- For example, the story starts when a woman's husband collapses and dies.

- An Inspiring Quote – this hooks the audience by making them wonder how the quote applies to the story they're about to read. Any quote that has something to do with the story can be used for short stories. For longer, narrative stories, a quote from someone within the story works best. If the story is about your mother, then quoting a phrase she frequently used can hook the reader, establish the theme of the book, and give an idea of what your mother was like.

- For example, the story starts with a man sitting at the bus stop. "Mama always said, 'Life is like a box of chocolates. You never know what you're gonna find.'"[3]

- A Startling Fact – this is similar to the Unusual Situation category. Use a fact that applies to the story you are writing. The kind of facts you use should reflect the mood of your story. If the story is meant to be fun and light-hearted, then stay away from shocking facts that are dark and grim in nature.

- For example, the story starts with quoting the fact that children from single-parent homes are 17% more likely to drop out of school. And 1 in 5 children are likely to have difficulty graduating from high school. This is a great start for a memoir that focuses on the problems teens face.

Take a look at the Easy-Peasy Story Guide you completed for the current story. Which of the hooks shown above works best with the answers you gave on the story guide? Who are you writing about?

---

3 *Forrest Gump*. Directed by Robert Zemeckis, Paramount Pictures, 1994.)

Did that person have an inspirational quote that seemed to define who they were? Or perhaps it was a quote that inspired you in some way and you can start by listing the quote and then adding your reaction to it.

Another method is to find the moment that best expresses the message you want readers to gain from this story. What's the first obstacle that relates to this moment? Let the readers know what goal, or ideal, is important to the person you are writing about and why it's important. Then hit them (the readers and the person in the story) with whatever obstacle that threatens to block the goal, dream, or ideal.

You can also hook them with the reason you're writing this book. If you want to increase the reader's awareness about a situation you've experienced, you might want to start with a question, a mystery, a startling fact, or even an event that inspires dread. For example, a cancer survivor might start off a story like this:

> I stared at the doctor, my mouth hanging open, "Ovarian cancer. How bad is that?"
>
> "Only four in ten women survive," Dr. Stevens said, as he fidgeted with his clipboard.

Now, that's a hook. This story starts with the very moment the patient finds out she has cancer. Two hooks are used in this example, a startling fact and the dread factor. The story could then move on to introduce all the elements that are part of the beginning of a story.

IN THE BEGINNING

All stories, no matter where in the world they are told, tend to have the same structure. It has been that way for, at least, as long as humans have recorded stories. Audiences expect stories to follow the established pattern. And that starts with . . . the beginning.

The beginning of a story accomplishes several important tasks for both the reader and the writer. Knowing what each section of the story does will help you decide which events to include and where to place them.

Establish Setting

The beginning tells readers when and where a story takes place. Details that establish the setting give the audience clues of how to understand the story. People living in 1880 have a much different view on life than do the people born in the last twenty years. Technology, historic events, and social trends all affect how the people in the story think, act and speak.

Some events are easier used to establish the setting than others. A move to a new neighborhood is a good example. Explaining why the family plans to move gives the reader an idea of the emotional, social, or economic setting of the story. Describing the new house and neighborhood gives the reader the physical setting. And any mention of a historical event that happens at the time of the move gives the reader a sense of when the story takes place.

No matter what events you use to create the storyline, it's important to describe the setting as early as possible. What do the buildings look like? What clothes are the people wearing? What sorts of tools and machines does everyone use? What kinds of sounds can a person hear while walking down the street? What's the latest news headline that everyone is talking about?

This applies to small, family stories just as much as it does to bigger stories. What do the houses on your block look like? What do the rooms in your house look like? What clothes are the members of your family wearing? What kinds of tools, or toys, are located in any given room? What kinds of sounds can you hear from the living room? And what is the latest news headline, or gossip, that everyone is talking about?

The better you establish the setting, the more the readers are going to feel like they're in the actual story. Use as many of the five senses as possible. Describe sounds, colors, textures, smells, and even tastes. Use of any or of all of the senses makes the story come alive.

Introduce People

The beginning gives the readers their first glimpse at the people in the story. While it's important to create a mental picture of each person in the story, it's even more important to show the audience their personalities. Is Aunt Matilda tall, thin, and snarky while her sister is pleasantly plump with a charming personality to match? Is it obvious from the beginning that Joe and his brother Bill will eventually have a major disagreement over some minor problem?

Memoirs and family stories are about people. Make sure to take the time to introduce these people to the reader. What you communicate may be the only way future generations will have to get to know the people you are writing about. And isn't that the reason for writing family stories?

If you're worried about including details that will matter to the story, take a look at the events that unfold during the middle of the book. What are the characters doing? What arguments do they have? What mistakes do they make? Then add details to the beginning of the story that show why those later events were bound to happen.

Define Story Goals

Story Goals is a writing term. What it basically means is that someone wants, or plans, to do something. Stories benefit from having clearly defined goals that are shared with the reader. Robert wants to improve himself. It's a great ambition for Robert, but it doesn't give the reader any useful information. Change the goal to Robert wants to improve himself by losing 30 pounds and you have a way the readers can track Robert's progress throughout the story.

Why do the people in a story need goals?

Because tension is what makes a story interesting. We watch sports to see which team will score the most points. We watch action movies to see if the good guys can defeat the bad guys. And we watch romances to see if two strangers can overcome their differences in order to find true love.

The key to putting tension into your story is for your characters to have goals. Short stories tend to have smaller goals and longer stories tend to have one major goal, but can include several smaller ones as well. Goals are the way for the reader to gauge if the characters are winning or losing. Although, it might be more accurate to say that goals are the way the readers gauge which people in the story are winning and which ones are losing at any given time.

Since the events of your memoir, or family story, have already happened, picking out goals is one of the easier parts of writing a story. Take a look at the important events in the person's life and then go back in time. What circumstances motivated the person to work towards that event? What emotions prompted the person to make that decision? Both of those questions can be combined to create the goal for your story.

For example, during the summer, my dad worked mule teams in California to help support his siblings. My dad working mule teams in the summer is the event. His parents spending their money on drinking and gambling are the circumstances that motivated Dad to take such a difficult job. And his love for his younger siblings is what prompted him to make that decision. Put them together and I have a goal of my dad trying to earn enough money to feed his siblings while still attending school.

As you develop the story goal, ask yourself, who else was involved, what did they say, what needs made the goal necessary, and did they have an actual plan, or did they just react to the problems as they happened? Include any obstacles or challenges the people in the story expected to face as they worked towards the goal. All of these elements build tension in the story. They set the stage for the conflict that happens later.

Show Life Before Change

Good stories are all about change. People face obstacles. They overcome obstacles. Hopefully, they learn a lesson from their experience, and they change. Then, they tell others their story in the hopes of preventing family and friends from making the same mistakes.

In order for the story to work, you need to show what a person's life was like before things changed. Think about how different the person acted before the events described take place. You could compare how the person's financial situation changed or how their standing in the community improved or declined. Then pick a few events to show the reader those parts of the person's life before the change.

GOOD STUFF IN THE MIDDLE

The middle of a story is where all the cool stuff happens. It's filled with challenges the person in the story faces on their journey and explores the story goals. Movie previews are mostly material from the story's middle. Those visual snippets show the viewers why they want to see the movie, or read the book. For a comedy those are images of people acting silly or placed into ridiculous situations. Horror relies on images that generate shock and terror. A documentary about a famous musician will show images of screaming fans, stage performances, and possibly arguments among the band members in order to interest a potential audience.

Take a moment and picture what the movie trailer for your story would look like. If you have difficulty picturing this, try imagining how the movie poster, or book cover, would look. What scenes come to mind when you think about your story? Those are the events that make up the middle.

A heart-warming story about a person's battle with cancer creates images of hospitals, treatment sessions, and adjusting to the side-effects of the medical routines that are intended to save the person's life. Scenes that involve how the illness affect the person, family, friends, and coworkers are at the heart of the story and belong here.

Once you have an idea of what events belong in the middle of your story, move on to the next stage. Which is building suspense.

CONFLICT IS NOT A BAD WORD

"Happy families are all alike; every unhappy family is unhappy in its own way."[4]

What Leo means by his statement is that readers are not interested in the happy, mundane details that are familiar to all of us. Readers want to experience lives different from their own. And they want to watch as the people in a story face challenges and have their spirits tested. This is known as . . . *conflict*. Conflict makes stories interesting.

But using the word *conflict* seems to conjure images of punching someone in the face or people screaming at one another. Rather than focusing on these two limited and violent forms of conflict, let's use the term "struggles" instead.

---

4 Leo Tolstoy, *Anna Karenina*, 1878, published by The Russian Messenger.

The middle of the story is all about complications that result in struggles. Since memoirs and family stories are based on real events, you will want to look for the challenges the person faced as they worked towards their goal--the story goal.

> What obstacles stood in the way of the person reaching their goal?
>
> What events made the original situation worse?
>
> What actions by other people in the story made it harder to achieve the goal?
>
> Did the person in the story have personal limitations that made the goal more difficult?

All of these problems fall into the category of external struggles. These are mostly physical challenges. Struggles that take place outside the person's body as opposed to a mental or emotional conflict.

But there are also internal struggles. The character in the story might struggle to avoid the temptation of some addiction. It might be a struggle to make a decision, like picking one girl over another to marry. The person might struggle to face a situation they fear. And a person can even struggle to solve a mystery, like why a parent still had a picture of an old flame hidden in their belongings.

Here's an example, my grandmother discovered she had cancer when my mother was still in high school. A story about how my mother was affected by the event would include many complications to my mother's life because of the situation. During an interview with my mother, she mentioned several obstacles, during that time, that made it tougher to graduate from school.

- She had to take a job to help support the family.

- When she didn't make enough money at the first job, she had to find a second one.

- She was expected to take care of the other children since she was the oldest.

- She had to study hard to maintain her grades.

- And most of all, she worried about whether her mother would survive.

A more detailed interview would probably reveal that each of these challenges had several roadblocks along the way. Learning a new job presents a set of struggles all by itself and personality conflicts are bound to set in. Things never go the way they should, especially at work. The amount of time my mother spent working, studying, and taking care of the house and her mother created a physical challenge that left her exhausted. All of these are complications for just the first obstacle listed above.

The middle of the story is also about seeing the good in the situation. Don't focus on only the negative events, make sure to include the lucky breaks--the help the person received from others, and the moments of inspiration. Our lives are a series of ups and downs that all contribute to what we finally become. Exploring the highs and lows, we encounter on our journey, is what makes a story worth telling.

There's room for happy stories too. While many of the story examples in this book discuss serious matters, it's perfectly alright to write about the happy and joyous events a family experience. But even these light-hearted stories should include obstacles. Some obstacles are funny. Some are romantic. Still yet, others are inspirational. The same rules apply. Just keep the tone of the story positive.

END OF THE ROAD

The amazing part of our real-life journeys is what we learn along the way. That's what the end of the story is all about. Readers want to see how the person in the story has grown from the experiences they encountered as part of the efforts to achieve the story goal.

Once again, we're going to look at the events that really happened and use them for the story ending. Interview the person in the story for the following elements:

- What eventually made it possible to achieve your goal?

- Did you have to take a different approach to the problem in order to succeed?

- What lessons did you learn along the way?

- Describe the moment when you finally achieved your goal.

The story doesn't end as soon as the person completes their goal. The outcome not only affects the person who achieved the goal, but the lives of others as well. Write a few pages which show how the lives of the people involved are different from the beginning of the story. You can use the following questions as a guide.

- How did achieving the story goal affect the lives of the people involved?

- How did the main character react to the success? What were their thoughts?

END WITH A TWIST

Readers also like to end a story with a surprise. Is there something funny or unexpected that happened that relates to the story goal or the events of the story? Like two brothers who both want their father's old car as a keepsake. Then once the matter is settled, they find out that their dad hated the thing. Life is stranger than fiction and often provides a twist to a story if you take the time to look for one.

RETURN OF THE STORY GUIDE

The Easy-Peasy Story Guide has four questions you want to keep in mind as you decide which events to use in the beginning, the middle, and the end of your story.

> *⌀* What do you want the audience to know about the person in your story?

If the purpose of your story is to leave a record of how your father pioneered the industry in which he worked, then you want to pick events and moments that describes the journey. The beginning of the story should be filled with events about what motivated him to work in that field. The middle of the story should show the challenges he faced during his career. And finally, the end of the story is the place to showcase his accomplishments and how they affected himself and others.

Beginning, middle, end, all focused on what you want your audience to know.

> *⌀* Why are you writing this story?

A story meant to share the memory of someone you love needs to have plenty of details and use events that give a feel for what that person was like. If your reason for writing the story is to influence future generations, about something you feel strongly about, then it needs to have discussions and events that support your thoughts on the topic. Choose events based on whether you want to inform, persuade, entertain, or provide a historic guide along with your story.

   ✐   What tone do you want for your story?

Happy stories should obviously include plenty of happy events. A sad story will have more events that focus on the difficult or tragic portions of a person's life. Scary. Silly. Whatever tone you decide upon, the story will need events which fit within its category.

   ✐   What message do you want to share with your reader?

When a reader has finished your story, they should walk away with some sort of message or knowledge. They should feel like they learned something. It can be as simple as finding out that grandpa believed that hard work could solve any problem. The story needs events that demonstrate the message to the reader. Start with a goal, introduce a problem, and then show the reader how the person in the story worked towards that goal, all with your message in mind.

START SIMPLE

Creating a storyline can be one of the most daunting tasks in writing a story. But don't stress. Don't overthink it. Start simple.

Work on selecting three events to represent the beginning of your story. Just three. You can do that. Think of an event that will hook the readers. Then think about something that happened during the early part of the story, an event that stands out as extra interesting. Finally, pick an event that will explain the story goal. Show what the person in the story did when they chose this goal.

Include an event that creates a problem or an obstacle to obtaining the story goal.

Boom. You have a three-event start for your story. But, don't be surprised if several more events come to mind as you think about filling-out the beginning.

For example: *The Milkman's Son* starts with my dad dreaming of his dead ancestors. That event is intended to hook the readers. Then the story describes the family history research process. It explains my passion for finding where William "The Immigrant" Lindsey was born, which explains one of the story goals. And finally, the story describes my decision to take a DNA test to help my research efforts, which results in the discovery that my dad is not my biological father. This event created the main problem of the story. How to deal with the discovery of a previously unknown family.

Middles and endings can be just as simple.

For the middle, think of five obstacles that stood in the way of the person in the story reaching their goal. Then include the event where the person finally comes up with a solution.

Once again, using *The Milkman's Son* as an example: five obstacles that stood in the way of dealing with the discovery of my previously unknown family were:

1) my own preconceptions of what it meant to be family

2) concern over how the family I grew up with would react to the news

3) fear that the dad I grew up with would reject me

4) concern over whether my biological father would accept me

5) the difficult process of accepting strangers as family

Use three more events for the end of your story.

- ∅ One event that shows the person succeeding at the story goal.

- ∅ Another event to show how all the people in the story were affected by the success.

- ∅ And finally, an event that sums up how the person in the story feels and how it relates to the message you want the readers to know.

These three events work best if they occur in the same order as I have listed them.

In *The Milkman's Son*, a Thanksgiving dinner with my New Jersey family was the event I used to show how I learned to deal with the discovery of my new family members. Then I used the flight home as an event where I reviewed the adoption of my two youngest children. They are an important part of my journey throughout the story and are part of what I learned from the experience. The final event involved visiting my dad in Arizona. That's where the story started and it was a perfect place to deliver my final message to the readers. It's not blood that makes us family . . . it's the love that we share.

Simple.

SHORTER STORIES

Not everyone interested in family stories wants to write an entire book. You might have an anthology in mind or perhaps, a short story or two. No problem. The above method can be used for short stories.

Instead of writing entire chapters for each part of your story, write paragraphs. A short story will still have a beginning, middle and end. Write three paragraphs for the beginning of your story using the same structure as above. One paragraph to hook the reader and establish the setting. Another paragraph to describe something the person in the story needs. And then write a third paragraph that identifies the story goal and what the person in the story plans to do first.

The middle of story is still about obstacles standing in the way. Select three obstacles or even three examples of what happened during this time. For each of these challenges, write a paragraph describing the obstacle or challenge, another paragraph showing the actual struggle, and then a third paragraph explaining how the person in the story dealt with the challenge.

Then use three more paragraphs for the end of the story. One where the goal is resolved. A second to show how it affected the lives of the people in the story. And then a third paragraph where the person in the story expresses their thoughts and emotions about the situation

Easy-Peasy.

Keep in mind that this is a guideline. If you feel inspired to write more than a paragraph for any of these sections . . . please, do so. Write as much as you like.

LIFE WITHOUT CHALLENGE

The Easy-Peasy Method is intended to help people write a wide variety of family stories. In some cases, the purpose of a story might be to show what a person was like, or what the relationship was like between two people. Maybe you just want to write about how grandma and grandpa met, fell in love, and eventually got married, skipping past any problems or challenges they may have faced along the way.

Maybe you want to focus only on the good and positive moments in a person's life. Perhaps it might be a struggle for you to find the conflict in some situations. Either way, if you want to stay away from struggles, challenges, and conflict you can simply use instances. Follow the advice in this chapter and whenever a struggle, obstacle, or challenge is listed, find an event that serves as an example of what you want people to know.

Was grandpa not interested in grandma originally? Then include a few instances that show his initial reluctance to date her. Maybe your grandparents were neighbors in a small town and you want to show what life was like in that environment. Write about a few instances of small-town life. In order for this method to work, you will really need to have a strong idea of what you want the readers to know.

Stories that feature people facing challenges are stronger, but this method will work to create cute and informative tales about your family.

TEMPLATES

Choosing a story goal and then finding the complications that are necessary to create suspense can be a difficult task. If you find that you're struggling to create a storyline on your own, you can always use a template. They provide a plug-and-play option for storytelling. Here are a few templates to help you outline your story.

Template One – Three Obstacles

The idea behind this template is that once you decide on the story goal, you select three obstacles that stand in the person's way.

1. Introduction – write about the event that results in the person deciding they want to accomplish the story goal.

2. Setting – write about an event that brings other people into the story. This is about giving a sense of when and where the story takes place and who is involved.

3. First Struggle/Obstacle – write about an obstacle that stands in the way of achieving the story goal. It doesn't have to actually be the first complication the person faced, but it can be the first interesting obstacle that caused a problem. What is it about this obstacle that made it more difficult to obtain the story goal?

4. First Challenge Met – write about how the person dealt with the obstacle and what effect the experience had on the situation. Did this event leave the person closer, or farther, from reaching the story goal? Who helped and who worked against the person during this time?

5. Second Struggle/Obstacle – write about an obstacle that stands in the way of achieving the story goal. What is it about this obstacle that made it more difficult to obtain the story goal?

6. Second Challenge Met – write about how the person dealt with the obstacle and what effect the experience had on the situation. Did this event leave the person closer, or farther, from reaching the story goal? Who helped and who worked against the person during this time?

7. Third Struggle/Obstacle – write about an obstacle that stands in the way of achieving the story goal. What is it about this obstacle that made it more difficult to obtain the story goal?

8. Third Challenge Met – write about how the person dealt with the obstacle and what effect the experience had on the situation. Did this event leave the person closer, or farther, from reaching the story goal? Who helped and who worked against the person during this time?

9. Success/Failure – write about what eventually happens. Does the person do something different that allows them to finally succeed? Does the person have a change of mind and decide to do something else instead? Because this is real life, and not a movie made to delight audiences, there's a chance that the person in the story doesn't succeed in reaching their goal.

10. Wrapping It Up – write about how the events in the story impacted the person in the story and those around them. Include a final message to the reader that wraps-up what you want them to know.

Template Two – Ten Key Moments

This template is ideal for a story that's meant to be a record of a person's life. It focuses less on a story goal and more on ten amazing events in the person's life. Ten events that were important to the person in the story. Of course, if you can find a way to link all of the events to a single message, or a single goal, then the story will be better for it.

1. Introduction – write about the earliest moment the person can remember. Include as many details as possible to give the readers a sense of when and where the story takes place.

2. Event #2 – write about the most important event that happened during the person's early years. This should be an event that had a major impact on the person's adult life. Perhaps a lifelong friend, a debilitating injury/illness, or even a lesson that forever shaped the way he/she thought.

3. Event #3 – write about the person's first major event as an adult. This might be starting a career, marrying a spouse, or a major decision that marked a turning point in his/her life.

4. Event #4 – write about another major event. Possibilities include: a major accomplishment at work, a major accomplishment at home, a decision that moved the person's life in a new direction, a disaster or an injury, or the death of a loved one.

5. Event #5 – follow the same guidelines as event #4 above. Each of these should be an event that the person feels was important to them and one of the reasons they turned out the way they did.

6. Event #6 – follow the same guidelines as event #4 above.

7. Event # 7 – follow the same guidelines as event #4 above.

8. Event #8 – follow the same guidelines as event #4 above.

9. Event # 9 – follow the same guidelines as event #4 above.

10. Event # 10 – write about the last major event of the person's life. If the person is still alive, write about the latest major event that has happened to them. Then see if you can tie all of the events together with a thought, or piece of advice, the person has gained from these experiences.

Template Three – Six Major Turning Points

This template is meant to show how the person's life changed and went in an entirely new direction. It represents the zig-zag nature of our lives and how we should really expect the unexpected.

1. Normal - write about an early event in the person's life. A time when the person felt their life was pretty normal. As with the beginning portion of any story, include details that give the reader a sense of when and where the event takes place. This is also a good spot to share a few reflections the person has about their youth.

2. Turning Point #1 – write about the first event that changed the person's life, sending it in a new direction. This could be a move across the country, a disaster, or the divorce of his/her parents.

3. Turning Point #2 – once again, write about an event that changed the person's life.

4. Turning Point #3 – follow the same guidelines for Turning Point #2 above.

5. Turning Point #4 - follow the same guidelines for Turning Point #2 above.

6. Turning Point #5 - follow the same guidelines for Turning Point #2 above.

7. Turning Point #6 - follow the same guidelines for Turning Point #2 above.

8. Journey's End – write about what the person's life is like now. If the person is deceased, then write about what his/her life was like at the end. Include a few gems of what the person thought about life in general.

Template Four – Snapshots

This template is meant to give the readers a look into the personal moments of whoever you are writing about. Each section is a question from the Insightful category in the Interview chapter.

1. Write about an event that happened at the person's favorite place.

2. Write about the event that inspired the person's favorite story.

3. Write about an event that represents the one thing the person wants people to remember about him/her.

4. Write about the scariest event that happened to the person.

5. Write about the most embarrassing event that happened to the person.

6. Write about the funniest event that happened to the person.

7. Write about the event that involved the hardest decision the person had to make.

8. Write about the event that involved the hardest challenge the person ever faced.

9. Write about the event that involved something that few people know about them.

10. Write about the event that represents the most important lesson the person learned and wants to pass on to others.

That's it. Once you've gathered the information about the events you want to use in your story, you'll be ready for the fun part of writing. The actual writing.

NOTES

NOTES

BRINGING YOUR STORY TO LIFE

Memoirs and stories about family members who are still living allow you find out what the person thought about a situation and how they reacted to an event. That option isn't available for stories about ancestors who have long since passed away. Without the ability to interview ancestors from previous centuries, any stories about them will be short on personal details.

The challenge in this situation is to create an interesting story around limited or even unreliable details about their life. In some cases, you may only have estimates of the dates for the important events in the person's life.

FACTS VS FICTION

Family history research is about the collection of facts. Most of the time the result is a collection of dates with a few names attached. That's fine if you happen to be a genealogist, but if you want the rest of your family (the vast majority of your family) to take an interest in these facts you need to turn them into a story.

There are ways to use facts to add flavor to a story, but at a certain point some of these methods become creative fiction attached to a real story. This is known as Creative Non-fiction. Facts alone won't tell the whole story. Think of creative non-fiction as filling in the blanks.

It will be up to you to decide where on the fact versus fiction scale you want your story. You can write the story about your immigrant ancestor making the trip to America in 1800, using only the facts. Many of the methods in this chapter will help make that account more interesting.

The other option is to include elements that you create. Readers will probably appreciate a story where you include what you think it would be like to be in the situations you write about. Just make it clear to the reader, you are inserting yourself into the story, so the thoughts, reactions, and musings belong to you and are not part of any research source.

JUST THE FACTS

This section covers methods that are helpful for those who only want to include factual information in their story. These methods can also be used for stories that make use of creative non-fiction elements.

IT'S ALL IN THE DETAILS

One of the keys to writing a more interesting family history is to use details that will let others feel as if they know the person in the story. Details like being born on the ship crossing the ocean, operating the first lumber mill in the area, or having two children die during the potato famine add flavor to the otherwise dry facts about an individual.

Here are some details that you can use to bring your facts to life:

One-Word – if you have information that reveals what the person was like, then come up with one word that best describes them. Then look for information and stories that are examples of that trait. Use the word in your story and words that are similar in meaning.

Example:

> The Anderson brothers were roamers. Maybe the trait ran in the Anderson blood. Few members of the family seemed inclined to stay in one place. William Anderson eventually ended up in Washington with the bulk of the family. Bud died in a motorcycle accident while driving across the country.

Comments my mother has made about her father and uncle often discuss how both men had a difficult time staying in one place. They had a fondness for motorcycles and my grandfather was working in a gas station at the time he died. I know very little about the man, but I could use my one-word description to craft a story out of the few details that I do have.

Description – tell the readers what the person looked like and how they dressed. A few sources, like the WWI draft records, provide a limited description of the person. If no pictures or descriptions are available, research the kinds of clothing that were being worn in the place and at the time you are writing about. You can also look at census records for the person's occupation and use a description that's typical for someone doing that kind of work, at that time.

Example:

> Nancy Lindsay donned her blue, calico dress. The light cotton material was a good choice for the hot summer day ahead. Full around the skirt with large tucks and broad hems, the dress wasn't as stylish as the ones the ladies wore back east, but it served its purpose. And it was pretty in its own simple way.

Note how the example doesn't rely on knowing too much about Nancy. The dress description is standard for 1830 Ohio. A tiny bit of liberty has been taken by stating that she owned a dress like this and that it was pretty in its own simple way. Nancy may have hated calico or the style of the dress. These general statements are more about weaving historically accurate details into the story than they are a statement of Nancy's personal tastes.

Habits – depending on the sources that are available, you can draw upon a person's habits to add color to the story. Include any phrases the person commonly used. Write about any hobbies the person had. Research the details of that hobby for bits you can include in the story. Include a description of what tools and equipment are used in the hobby and how they were used. This isn't so much a statement that your ancestor did things in exactly this manner, but more of an example of the standard way they were done. The method is meant to give the reader a feel for what life was like for someone in the same situation.

Example:

> *Albert Lindsay Jr. stepped out of the office into the hot Arizona sun. More than forty cars were parked on the small lot where he worked. His tiny office sat in the middle of a paved lot that was only half the size of other used car lots on the block, but no one was visiting any of them on a blistering day like today. Al pulled a pack of Lucky Strikes out of his shirt pocket and lit a cigarette, holding it between his thumb and forefinger.*

This is a detail that I happen to remember about my grandfather. He smoked for as long as I can remember. His home and clothes smelled of smoke. Even though this is a memory, the same thing could be done for a person you never met as long as you have a few of the details. All you would need to know to write a section like this is that the person smoked, the brand of cigarettes smoked, and that they sold used cars from a small lot in Arizona.

A Day in the Life – based on the occupation, the place where the person lived, the person's religion, and any other known facts, describe the typical events that were part the daily occurrence. What steps were necessary to dress in the fashion of the day? What tasks did they do as part of their daily job duties? What was the normal routine for a family at dinner time?

Example:

> *William Lindsay rolled up his sleeves as he walked out to the forge. He lifted his leather apron from where it hung from a hook on one of the wooden posts that supported the roof of the smithy. Then he grabbed the well-used tongs and hammer from his workbench. Another day of pounding metal lay ahead of him.*

Note how the only thing you would need to know in order to write this section is that William Lindsay worked as a blacksmith. These are standard details for a blacksmith in the 1800's. An entire section could be written about William working in the smithy. Unless you have a reason to believe that the person you are writing about was responsible for inventing an innovation in their industry, a standard description of the work is probably quite accurate for what an average day was like.

Countries, Cities, and Other Places – locations provide some of the best details for a story because they will be the same for everyone. Big Ben looks the same to anyone who sees it. Of course, the description will be different based on who writes about it, but that's another matter. Research the country, state, town, and street where the person lived. Include landmarks and other important locations in the area. Describe them in a way that will make readers feel as if they are there.

Example:

> *John Lindsay rode into West Union on Mulberry Street. Grimes and Company owned the first lot on the left. It was a large plot with a pond in the middle. John passed East Street, Pond Street, and Pleasant Street before he finally reached the court house.*

The description of West Union is based on a map of the town. Street names, business names, and in some cases the name of the proprietors might all be found on the map itself. Talking about them in relation to one another gives a sense of being there.

Businesses and Schools – both of these institutions are much more likely to have information about them than your average person living in the location where they're found. That makes them a great source for details to bring your story to life. Research these institutions and include the names of people who were involved during the time you are writing about. Who owned the company? What was the name of the teacher at the school? What kind of business did the business do? Which countries did the children in the school immigrate from and what languages might they speak? What's been written about these institutions in papers, journals, books, and other historical documents?

Example:

> *John Lindsay rode into Bentonville and stopped in front of his brother's business. James had specialized in wagon making rather than your average, run-of-the-mill blacksmith like John. The injury John suffered during the Civil War made it difficult to mount and dismount from his horse, but he eventually managed to hit the ground still standing. A sign was posted on the outer wall of the building. "James Lindsey. Wagon maker. All kinds of repairing done in this line."*

Because James ran a business in town, it was easier to find information about his wagon making activities than it was to find information about him. Business directories are fairly common and usually list the address, name of the proprietor, and the kind of business. In this case, the entry for James' business indicated he did repairs as well. If you're willing to allow a little creative content in his story, it would be an easy matter to write a section where John talks shop with James or has come over for some advice on a project.

Churches and Organizations – both of these represent social activities. Things that people did when they weren't busy earning a living, makes great details for giving the reader a better idea of what the person in your story might be like. These institutions represent the opinions and views of the people who belong to them. In many cases, they can provide a list of events and actions that the person in your story probably attended and participated in.

Example:

> *Like many of the Irish that had immigrated to North America, the Lindsay's were Presbyterian. The congregation met in a stone building in West Union. Reverend John P. Vandyke led the congregation. There seemed to be more members than space within the church. Members discussed and then voted on expanding the size of the building to 50x60. Some of the elders discussed rumors of another church being formed in Eckmansville, seven miles away. More than a few of the elders thought the creation of another church so near to theirs might weaken the congregation.*

All of the items in the example are based on historical facts taken from *Caldwell's Atlas of Adams County*. When written like this, they sound more like a story than statistics. A couple of liberties were taken with the information. "More members than space," is a reasonable expectation based on the fact that they expanded the size of the building. And nothing in Caldwell's Atlas is mentioned about "rumors" of another church. The source only states that a second Presbyterian church was built in Eckmansville. If there weren't rumors about the building of another church it would have to be the first time in the history of the world that no one in a town commented about new construction.

Wealth and Influence – these kinds of details affect how a person may have dressed, what they probably ate, and which activities they were most likely to do. It also gives the writer an idea of how to write the descriptions. A poor woman wearing her Sunday best to church may simply be in a dress that is the least worn of the one or two that she owns. While a wealthy woman is more likely to be wearing the latest fashion of the day. The kind of words you use in your description should reflect the amount of money the person had and the level of influence of their friends.

Example:

> *Grace and Maxine Anderson rose before the sun to start preparations for Thanksgiving dinner. Max, having slightly more money than Grace, had bought a small turkey. Grace did her best to provide enough potatoes, green beans, and a few oranges to feed the two sisters and all their children. No part of the turkey went to waste. The innards, diced and mixed with a little flour, made a delicious gravy. Max boiled the neck to make stock and then to be eaten during the meal. It wasn't much, but at least the two families could celebrate the holiday with reasonably full bellies.*

Most of the elements of this section come from stories my mother told me combined with my own early memories about Thanksgiving. But this section works for almost any family struggling at the poverty level. A story about the grandparents on my dad's side would look much different. Both of them came from well-to-do families and had servants to help with the cooking. Food was abundant as was cigarettes, alcohol, and friends who disappeared around the time my grandparents spent the last of their money.

Size of Family – the number of people in a family and their ages can help add life to a historical story. Actions and responses appropriate for someone that age can make the description of the family more vivid. Perhaps little Suzie is still in diapers and has to be fed at dinner time. Four teenage boys crowded into a single room creates a memorable image. And children of all sizes doing chores appropriate for their age provides a look at what life was like during the time you are writing about.

Example:

> *Margaret Lindsay skipped outside to find eggs. Inside the house, Mama was busy cooking breakfast. John was a year younger than her, but because he was a boy he didn't have to tend to the chickens. He carried water to the house instead.*

Even though the ages aren't listed here, it's obvious that Margaret's skipping and her use of the word "Mama" tells the readers that she is young. Comparing ages between her and John gives the reader a better sense of the people as a family. All of this information is based on census data, but it reads like a story and will be much more entertaining to future audiences.

What's for Dinner? – food is a major part of our everyday lives. What people eat. How they prepare it. What it tastes like. The vast number of cooking shows currently on television and the internet are proof that what people eat is a topic of interest. Here again, research the foods that were common for the time, place in your story and then describe it. There's no guarantee that the people you are writing about ate this exact meal, but this is more of an observation of the times than a statement of historic fact.

Example:

> *John Lindsay walked past the hotel Moses Buck operated. A bill tacked on the outside wall listed the meals available inside for the week. Corn bread, cold bread, stew, and boiled eggs for breakfast. Soup, poultry, cutlets, and vegetables for dinner. They even had dessert. Pie and coffee. Then for tea, Moses offered light hot bread, cold bread, fish, and stewed fruit.*

Moses Buck operated a hotel where John lived in 1853. But the "Bill of Fare" is from a book published during the same year . . . in Philadelphia. My records don't mention a bill of fare or if the hotel even served food. It may not be possible to find the exact information needed. However, by combining the information from both of these sources, I have created a reasonably accurate snapshot of what it may have been like in West Union, Ohio during 1853.

Ten types of details are listed in this section. If you think of more, then use the same methods as above to turn dry facts into vivid images of the past. It isn't necessary to use all ten detail types. Take the ones that you feel will work best to tell the kind of story you want to write and then leave out the rest. Or use the details that you find the easiest to write. Do whatever works best for you.

"What will happen if I use all ten detail types?"

Your story will be filled with all sorts of interesting information that brings it to life. You will have also have crammed an incredible amount of historical facts into a story in a way that's fun to read. Plus, you will have greatly increased the size of your story. If you wrote a few paragraphs for each detail and had ten events you wanted to write about . . . that'd be dozens of pages of *story* with each part telling about a different aspect of the person's life.

HISTORICAL SOURCES

The kinds of details you can find in a historical source depends on the kind of record you search through. Each one gives some details that you can use to create a more vivid story for your readers. Here is a list of records and the details you are likely to find in them.

- Census Records – the information available changes from census to census, but can have an amazing amount of information; place of residence, occupation, everyone who lives in the household and their relationship, marital status, the number of years married, birth location, birth location of parents, value of real estate owned, value of personal estate owned, number of months unemployed, highest level of education, year of immigration, number of years in the United States, own or rent house, farm schedule, and special conditions like blind, deaf, mute, insane, idiotic, pauper, criminal, or illiterate.

- Agriculture Schedules – if the family owned a farm, this resource provides a great many details about the family; farm acreage, farm value, fences, labor, cattle and their products, sheep, pigs, and number of acres for each type of crop.

- Tax Records – the details from these records include level of wealth, occupation, location, and the nature of the property owned. The information in this record can give you a clue about the amount of wealth the person had and what kind of details would be appropriate for their story. In other words, a poor person's story will have a different set of descriptions than a rich person's story.

- Land Records – size of lot, location, and the same information for the surrounding area.

- Wills/Probate Records – in addition to mention of guardianship of minors, these records provide estate inventories that you can use to write descriptions of the homes, knowing that these items existed in the residence.

- Birth Records – names, birth date, birth location, names of parents, and sometimes lists if the mother was married.

- Marriage Records – names, date of the event, event location, names of witnesses, and sometimes lists if the couple was married by a judge in a court rather than a church.

- Death Records – names, birth and death date, residence, nearest relative, names of parents, and cause of death. Knowing how the person died gives you a detail that you could use at the end of your story. Although, this may be a detail too gruesome for some.

- Church Records – these records include baptisms, marriages, and funerals that give the date and location of the event, name of the church, and often sponsors/witnesses that were present. Other church records include: minutes, diaries, administrative records, and membership records.

- Cemetery Records – information given to the cemetery by whomever made the funeral arrangements can include: name, birth and death dates, names of relatives, religious affiliation, military service, country of origin, and other person details.

- Obituaries – really, what can't you find out about a person from an obituary? These often include real stories about the person's life and can even serve as an outline for the story you are writing. Obituaries often give insight into the personality of the deceased, making them a great source for ideas on how to portray the person.

- Military/Draft Records – these can often be an excellent source of physical descriptions for the person, giving height, weight, hair color, eye color, body type, and complexion. Name, age/birth date, city of residence, race, profession, employer, place of business, marital status, nearest relative, place of birth, and description. Pension and Service Records will include rank, dates of service, and identify the military unit in which the person served.

- Newspapers – there's no telling what kind of information might be found in a newspaper article, but you can be sure that whatever it is, it will add wonderful, colorful details to the story of this person's life. Awards, arrests, accomplishments, maybe even an Op Ed piece that gives you and the reader a glimpse of what went on inside the person's mind.

- Business Advertisements – it's easy to think that the only information a business advertisement might offer is the name and location of the business, the nature of the business, and possibly the name of the owner. But each advertisement has its own style that makes it stand apart from the competition and that provides you a glimpse at the owner's personality as well.

- Business Directories – not only will directories provide the owner's name, address of the shop, and the profession, but you can quickly find out what other businesses were on the same block. These may be people who the person in your story talked with on a daily basis. They might even be rivals.

- City Directories – these provide details about the person's name and address, but might also give you their occupation, religious affiliation, political affiliation, and marital status.

- Historical Books — books about the formation of a town, county, or state will usually have historical references to the important people and events in its early history. This includes: churches, cemeteries, military heroes, early settlers, and key events and figures. Even if they don't mention the person you're writing about, they are a rich source for details from that time period. Everything from who owned the general store to the first murder committed in the area.

- Biographies — these are often in the form of a *Who's Who* book. Highlights from a person's life are discussed and can are a rich source of details if your person is in the book. The kind of details that are included will be based on the reason why the person was included in the book. They might be an early settler to a region, or the owner of the only tavern for fifty miles, or a circuit judge.

- Police/Court Reports — the person in your story might be a plaintiff, defendant, witness, or juror. Records might be an adoption, a guardianship, a name change, a divorce, or a criminal case. Whatever the reason, any details that come from a court case are going to be interesting. All you have to do is mention police or a courtroom and you have grabbed the reader's attention.

- Ship Registers — these are great if you want to describe the journey across the ocean. The details include: the person's name, departure and arrival dates, port of departure, port of arrival, names of others on ship, ship name, birth date, and birth place. A little extra research here might reveal an exciting discovery. Did any of the people on the ship settle in the same town as the person you are writing about?

- Immigration Records — include name, date, address, occupation, date of arrival or naturalization, and country of origin. Petitions for naturalization might also include names of witnesses. Border crossing documents also include amount of money on person, reason for visit, destination, apparent health, and port of arrival.

- Local Council Meeting Minutes – this is a great source for finding out what was happening in the community during the time the person lived there.

- Family History Societies – this is another treasure trove of information. You never know what you might find, and the biggest benefit is a lot of the research has already been done for you. Details might include: physical description of the area, descriptions of major landmarks, list of major events affecting the area, biographies of early settlers and anyone who had a major influence on the region, early drawings of the area, maps, and much more.

- Occupational Records – these records include: name, place, date, residence, work reference, occupation, and employer. These sources might also provide names of coworkers and products the company made or services the company provided.

- Workhouse and Union Records – aside from the standard information, these records can provide the reason why a family needed assistance, admissions of creed, and minutes from Board of Guardianship meetings.

- School/Alumni Records – these records include: names, teachers, fellow students, and any post-school events that the person may have attended. Plenty of year books are now available online.

- Voter Registration – in addition to the usual name, address, and year of residence, the registration will give the voting precinct, and political affiliation. Both of these items can lead to details based on the politics of the person in your story.

* Most of these records can be found on genealogical research sites, such as Ancestry.com, Family Search.org, and Find My Past.

HISTORIC EVENTS RATHER THAN HISTORICAL STATISTICS

Another method that focuses less on names, dates, and other vital statistics and embraces the story elements is historical events. The use of these events will draw your readers into the story so they are participating in what's happening rather than just reading about it. Historical events add an active and exciting background to the story you are telling. The use of historical events also connects the story to a time and place.

Select an important date for the person in your story, like a birth, a marriage, or the start of a business. Then search for historic events that happened in the same area, during that year. You can also use major events, like the Civil War. Events that don't take place in the area where the person in your story is located, but are large enough to impact a state or an entire country.

For example:

> In August of 1850, distilleries were the largest manufacturing industry in Tennessee, a fifteenth toll road was connected to Nashville, and Robert Williams was born in Williamson.

While the example is only a single paragraph, it was intended to make the information about Robert's birth more interesting, and the amount of detail given for each item could be expanded. Details can serve as colorful background to the real story and the story of the person you are writing about. You can use historic events in your story without turning it into creative non-fiction. Just observe the details of the event and avoid having the person in the story interact with them.

For example:

John Williams drove his cart north on the road to Franklin. Nashville had just added it's fifteenth toll booth, making it less profitable to sell his goods there. Besides, it was farther away. He crossed the tracks of the Decatur and Montgomery line, just at the edge of town.

Two heavily loaded wagons came down the road towards him. Each wagon was pulled by a pair of horses and had seven oak casks loaded in back. Four casks on the bottom and three more stacked on top of the others. The name of the Boyd family distillery was printed on the lid of each barrel.

Whiskey.

Many of the nearby farmers sold their excess corn to one of the local distilleries in order to purchase goods they needed from town. Of course, if a farmer had enough thirsty friends, he had the corn turned into whiskey and the distillery kept a portion of the product in payment. Then the farmer could sell the sour mash himself, making more money than he would have from selling the corn.

John tipped his hat as he passed the drivers in the whiskey wagons. Then he continued into town. The baby was on the way and he needed to fetch the doctor.

Notice how much the colorful details add to the story. Research about Williamson County in 1850 told me that whiskey- making was a major industry at the time and that the fifteenth toll road had been built on one of the routes into Nashville. A little more research revealed the facts about the whiskey industry and how most of the farmers were involved in one way or another. A map of Franklin from around that time period and an old picture of a wagon filled with whiskey casks gave me everything I needed to write the section above.

Compare that to the typical family history that tells the reader the name of the person, the place where the person was born, and in what year the event took place. One is giving the reader dusty, dry facts and the other is a story that will grab their attention.

Any other facts that you might want to include can be handled in the same manner, such as the event representing the birth of John and Sarah's first child. Rather than simply stating that Robert was the first child of John and Sarah Williams, details about whether it was common to have a doctor help deliver a baby during that time period, what babies wore, and the presence of family members based on the names taken from a local map of that time period.

Here is a list of historic events that can pull your reader into the story:

- News events such as wars, murders, natural disasters, and politics.

- Trends and fads that were popular at the time. Fashion. Phrases. Popular activities. Clothing. Hair styles. Hobbies.

- Movements. Any organized effort by a group to push forward an idea. Like prohibition.

- Social events. What did wealthy do in their spare time? What did commoners do?

- Business events. What businesses started? What changes or innovations were made in a local or national industry?

- Education events. Was a new school built? Did the school change curriculum?

- Religious events. Revivals. Brawls between congregations. New churches built.

PUTTING THE READER IN THE STORY

This method works for fiction and non-fiction alike. It has the greatest power to make readers feel as if they are actually in the story. And it's . . . easy.

Use the five senses as much as possible. Instead of telling readers what they see, describe it with colors, lighting, and visual textures. Include smells, and tastes, and sounds, and how things feel. Is it hot or cold? Do the wooden planks of a wagon feel rough and brittle, or new and smooth?

The more senses you use to describe things in your story, the better the reader can imagine it. And the more the reader can see, hear, smell, feel, and even taste the events you describe in your story, the more real it will be for them.

Example:

> *Grace opened the front door of her house and then walked outside. Paint that had been a brilliant white—twenty years ago—was now cracked, peeling, and discolored. The leaves on the large Black Walnut trees in the front yard were turning colors. Some still green, while others were yellow*

> *and orange. A gust of wind swirled bits of dead grass around her. The chill of an approaching storm cut through the holes in Grace's well-worn jacket, leaving her to shiver as she crossed the yard. She walked the two short blocks to Broadway, the town's busiest street. The scent of freshly baked bread drifted along the crisp autumn air, making her stomach grumble. A handful of coins is all she had to buy food for her family's dinner. Would that be enough? And what about tomorrow?*

CREATIVE NON-FICTION

Sometimes, the people in our stories are no longer around. We can't interview them to find out what they said or how they felt during an event in their lives. In this situation, you might want to use your imagination about what happened. If you're not comfortable creating events that resemble what might have happened, then you can stick with the methods for adding details that are described on the previous pages.

On the other hand, it's alright to include creative fiction as part of your story . . . as long as you let the readers know that's what you are doing. Readers, for the most part, are pretty accepting of this kind of family story. A story that contains the important facts about their lives, but includes your thoughts and reactions to the events. Or even a story where you write what you think are reasonable scenarios and dialogue based on the information you have gathered.

One of my ancestors is David McCord. He and his brother were captured by Indians during the French and Indian War. Eventually, they were turned over to the French at Fort Detroit., and taken up to what is now Canada. As part of a prisoner exchange program, they were shipped over to England and finally brought back to North America in time for the Revolutionary War.

No one knows every detail of David's experiences. There is no record of what David might have said to his brother on any given day. A story about all the amazing things he experienced would have to include a great deal of creative non-fiction to fill in the gaps. By imagining what he saw and what he might have said to the people around him, I could write a story that would give readers a reasonable idea of his experiences. Readers will have been educated about the known events and entertained as well.

If my story about the McCord brothers sounds like something you would like to read, then you can see how readers would be attracted to your own creative non-fiction story.

* The suggestions in this section work for pure fiction as well. Adding details about wealth, religion, local landmarks, or anything of the items discussed will bring any story to life whether it's non-fiction, creative non-fiction, or fiction. As you write your memoir or family history story, you may develop an interest in writing fiction. Using these methods will help.

PUTTING YOURSELF IN THE STORY

The best way to write creative non-fiction is to put yourself in the story. Tell about the events from your perspective. Use your own thoughts and reactions to write about the details you include in the story. What makes people care about any story is how the person reacts to what happens around them. Bind the reader to these stories through you.

Here are some suggestions for how to write creative non-fiction for your story.

Your Reaction – how did you feel about an event, detail, or historical fact when you first read about it? Did it shock you? Did it make you laugh? As you are researching a story, keep a record of your thoughts and feelings about the things you discover. This will give you an idea of how the person in the story might have reacted to what happened. Use your own thoughts as part of the story.

You can also use these reactions to determine the best emotion to use when writing about the event. If it made you angry, then include words and descriptions in that section that relate to anger. Words like simmer to describe the weather, or stomp to describe how someone walks. Describe someone as crossing their arms or sneering at a comment.

If you feel a certain way about an event, or detail, in your story, then there's a good chance that the person you're writing about did as well. But the most important reason for doing this is that the emotions and reactions will come across as genuine . . . because they are. These are your emotions and reactions and you will be able to write in a way that makes them personal.

A Question for Every Event – ask questions about every event or detail in your story. If the person in your story moved across the country, then ask yourself, "Why did they move?" And maybe, "Why did they move there?" If the person lived through a disaster, then ask yourself, "How did they make it through such a horrible event?" Or, "What was it like to experience that kind of disaster?"

Practice asking questions about each event in the person's life. Keep asking yourself questions about the event until you have at least five of them. Then pick the two questions that you feel the most strongly about and use the answers to them as part of your story. If you're really ambitious, you can write about all the questions you ask. This will certainly give you as much material for your story as you will need. And it will ensure that you have covered the event as thoroughly as possible.

Asking questions will help you determine what any given fact could mean in the life of the person you're writing about. How was it important to them? Or was it not important at all? How did it affect their everyday life?

For example, Lydia Lindsay was mentioned in the Society section of the newspaper and my story about her and John could include something like this:

> *Lydia Lindsay came home from Trinity church services. "John," she called out. "We were mentioned on the Society page of the Portsmouth Daily Times. John. John? Did you hear me?"*
>
> *"What did the paper say about us?" John asked.*
>
> *She stopped in front of the hallway mirror and adjusted her hair. "Just that Harold will be staying with us when he comes to visit."*

This section of the story could be expanded by asking a few questions. How did John feel about being part of the social elite in Portsmouth? How did that status affect the way John and Lydia lived? What kind of friends did the two of them have?

Here's a few sample questions you could ask yourself when dealing with facts and historical events and how they might have affected the person in your story.

- Marriage: How did they meet? Where did they meet? What was the wedding like? and Who was at the wedding?

- Occupation: Why did the person choose this job? What did the person do during a typical day's work? Were there any professional rivalries? Was the work profitable during that time and place?

- ◎ News Event: Did the news event personally affect the person? How did the person react to the news? How did the person hear the news (newspaper, grapevine, other)?

- ◎ Trends: Did the person follow fads and other trends? Could the person afford to follow fads and other trends? Did the person have a circle of friends that all followed the same fad or trend? Did the person talk about trends and fads to their friends?

- ◎ Play Time: As children, most of us pretended to be someone else. Cowboys, astronauts, pretty princesses, or even the child that went blind because our parents washed our mouths out with soap. Pretending is a useful skill when writing creative non-fiction.

Take a look at the facts, details, and events that were part of the person's life. Then try to imagine how each of those things affected the person and how they made them who they were. John Crawford Lindsay grew up in the frontier of Ohio. He and one of his brothers learned the blacksmithing skill. He fought in the Civil War and was wounded. His first wife died after only thirteen years of marriage. His second wife came from an affluent family and was a prominent figure in the high society circle of Portsmouth.

Now, use your powers of make-believe and pretend to be that person. You're still going to react to the facts, details, and events as yourself, but a version of yourself that has had the same experiences as the person in your story. How would you react to being part of high society after growing up as a blacksmith, fighting in a war, and dealing with a disability?

STORY EXAMPLE

"*Mayflower Bastard: A Stranger Among the Pilgrims*" by David Lindsey, is a good example of how to write a family story based on historical facts. If you're interested in giving creative non-fiction a try, then I suggest picking up a book like this to see how it can be done.

NOTES

NOTES

PUTTING TENSION INTO YOUR FAMILY STORY

C reating tension in your story was discussed previously, but it's an important enough element of storytelling to cover in a separate section. Tension is based on the anxiety that comes from uncertainty. While you want to avoid tension in real life, stories thrive on causing anxiety in your readers. Readers have a hard time putting down a story when they wonder what's going to happen next.

Goals are the key to creating tension in your story. As soon as a goal is put into a story, the reader wants to find out if the person you're writing about will succeed. It's the same reason people watch sports. In basketball, we watch to see if a player makes that three-point shot at the buzzer. In football, we watch to see if the team with the ball can score a touchdown, but we might be willing to settle for a field goal. In baseball, we watch to see if the pitcher can strike out the batter. Or if you're rooting for the other team, you watch to see if the batter can hit the ball and get on base.

The uncertainty of each of the above situations creates tension. Fans of the sports might hold their breath during the pitch. Or grab their friend's arm in a white-knuckled grip as the quarterback throws a pass. This tension is what makes sports so popular and the tension relies on the uncertainty of the team achieving their goal.

Everyone has goals. A goal is just something that we want to do. Babies want to eat, sleep, have their diapers changed, and be comforted in the arms of a loved one. As people grow older, their goals grow as well. As a teenager you might want to go to college or to play video games all day long. Adults may want to have children, change careers, or convince their spouses to help with dinner once in a while.

The people you're writing about had goals. They wanted to do something. In most cases, they struggled to get what they wanted. Obstacles stood in their way. The more important the goal, the more likely it is that a major obstacle threatened to prevent the person from getting what they wanted. Or maybe it wasn't a single, huge obstacle that stood in the way, but several small to medium size problems instead.

For your story, determine what the person you are writing about wants and then find out what was keeping that from happening. Here's what that goal and obstacle structure looks like in a story.

1) A person wants something.

2) Then some sort of obstacle makes it difficult, or even impossible, for the person to have what they want.

3) The person struggles to find a solution to the problem.

4) Every action the person takes either makes it easier, or harder, to get what they want.

   a) Readers are not sure if the action the person is taking will work. This creates tension.

   b) The anxiety readers feel because of this tension makes

them want to know what happens next

   c) Readers continue to read until this cycle is broken.

5) Eventually, the person gets what they want.

6) Repeat steps 1 through 5 as often as necessary to complete the story.

The majority of your story is about what the person wants and what prevents them from getting it. Descriptions help the reader to picture the story in their head, but the thoughts, actions, and conversations a person has should be about what the person wants.

If the person you are writing about is still alive, you can interview them and find out what goals they had. You can also ask them why the goal was important and how they felt about the situations that developed as part of the effort to achieve that goal.

However, if you haven't had a chance to interview the person in your story, you can just look at what they accomplished. Treat that event as a goal and write about the obstacles that stood in the person's way. Perhaps graduating from college was a goal the person had at one point. The road to graduation must have had several challenges that blocked the person's progress toward that goal. And since the person eventually graduated, they managed to find a way to overcome those obstacles.

That's your story. Write about those obstacles.

- What challenge did the obstacle represent?

- How did the obstacle(s) make it more difficult for the person to achieve their goal?

- How did the person feel about the obstacle and the struggles that resulted from it?

- What solution did the person in your story find to overcome the obstacle(s)?

- How did the struggle/challenge/obstacle change the goal or the person's view of the goal?

THE MANY FACES OF CONFLICT

There's that word again . . . Conflict.

All families have conflict because that's a part of life. It may help to think of conflict as the struggles or challenges we face every day. Feel free to focus on those two words whenever "conflict" is mentioned. The concept and the end results will be the same.

When conflict is mentioned, it's often associated with the use of direct, physical force. Violence is not the only form of conflict. There are a variety of ways to build tension besides threatening the person in the story with a beat-down. The kind of conflict and tension that's used in the story is based on the obstacles the person faces.

A story about a person's experiences in WWII most likely discusses violent conflict, but it can also include moments of emotional conflict over having killed an enemy soldier in order to stay alive. The same story could include environmental conflict as they struggle against starvation, sickness, or surviving the weather.

As soon as you have chosen which goal you want to write about, ask yourself the following questions.

- What kind of obstacle(s) stands in the person's way?

- How does the obstacle(s) hinder the person?

- How can I make it worse?

Look through this list and see which kind of obstacles stood in the way of the goal.

Rivalry – this is also known as Person vs. Person conflict. What that means is the person in your story and someone else are not getting along. The rival actively opposes the person in the story, making it difficult or impossible to achieve his/her goal.

- They may want the same thing (have the same goal). Like when two people are competing for the same job or two athletes compete to grab a thrown football.

- They may want different things, but only one of those things can happen. For example, a married couple might disagree on what to do with the old garage on the side of their property. The husband may want to fix-up the garage and turn it into a mancave while the wife might want to demolish the old eyesore of a building in order to make room for a flower garden.

- One person may simply want to stop the other from achieving their goal. Maybe the person in your story wants to run for Senior Class President and had someone else who was determined to prevent it.

- One person may want what someone else already has, a prized coin collection, a corner office, a best-friend relationship with the boss, or a spouse.

Example:

John Williams lived in Williamson County, Tennessee. Whiskey production was one of the major industries in the area for many years, making the region one of the most prosperous in the country. During the Civil War, Union troops took what they wanted from the towns and farms in the area. This pillaging ravaged the economic foundation of the region. It took the people in the region decades before they fully recovered. Then in 1910, prohibition banned the production of whiskey. A story about any of the William's family could easily include rivalry obstacles that stem from

> *the war itself, the ravaged landscape that resulted from soldiers looting, and prohibitionists, wanting to stop the whiskey industry.*

Environment – this is also known as Person vs. Nature conflict. In this sort of conflict, the person deals with the natural forces that are connected to their goal. Natural forces not only include deserts, storms, and volcanoes, but also the unstable nature of the stock market, the hazardous landscapes of a manufacturing floor, or the rules of survival in the world of real estate. These are all situations that provide obstacles which are a natural part of the environment.

- The weather works against the person and is often sudden and unexpected. Droughts, hurricanes, and natural disasters all provide obstacles created by Mother Nature. But a run on the stock market or a shortage of raw materials provide similar obstacles in the business world. Both sets of obstacles are a result of the natural environment working against the person and their goal.

- Harsh landscapes provide a sort of obstacle course for the person working towards a goal. This is different from the weather because a person can usually foresee the problems that a harsh landscape represents. Deserts will be hot and dry. A person wanting to cross the arid landscape will suffer if they aren't prepared for the harsh conditions. But the same is true for corporate, industrial, and technological landscapes. There will be elements that are part of the environment that require careful preparation and although with the appropriate precautions taken, the journey is still hard and potentially dangerous.

- Animals/Machines are similar to the Person vs. Person style of conflict. Animals in a nature setting and machines in a business setting can both cause problems to a person with a goal. This is different from the weather and harsh landscapes categories in that animals can react to what the person does and machines can be personified as if the conflict is a contest between man and machine.

🍃 Survival is not really a separate category, but it may be helpful to think of it as one. The difference is that in the three categories above, the forces listed threaten to stop the person from getting what he/she wants, but in a survival situation, the person's very life is in danger. And if the person dies, they aren't very likely to achieve their goal.

Example:

The living conditions in Ireland made it necessary, or at least desirable, to move to the United States. While William "The Immigrant" Lindsey survived the trip across the ocean, several of his wife's family died in a similar voyage a few years later. Once they arrived in America, they moved to the frontier of Ohio. A story about the Lindseys in early Ohio could easily include obstacles about the dangerous ocean terrain and the hazards of pioneer life, which include animals, hostile Indians, and survival.

Emotions and Desires – this is also known as Person vs. Self and is an internal conflict. In other words, the person struggles with an emotion, a desire, a decision or anything else that takes place within their own mind. This is not something that anyone else can see or feel. It's entirely possible that nobody else knows about the person's struggle.

- Important decisions like who to marry, what job to take, or which child to save from a burning building all create an internal struggle. While all obstacles include some element of this category, really important decisions can cause great stress before the person finally makes a choice. It's a good practice to try and find what decision the person struggled to make in order to overcome an obstacle.

- Desires can get in the way of what a person wants to do. Especially, in the case of addiction. Substance abuse can threaten the desire to be a good provider and have a happy family. Greed can stand in the way of friendship. Political ambition can be an obstacle to matters of the heart. Obstacles in this category involve the person struggling with themselves. Family histories are bound to be full of examples of this kind of obstacle. While not as serious a threat as you might want for your story, many of us struggle every day to eat healthy and avoid junk foods.

- Emotions are similar to desires. While desires represent a second goal that conflicts with all of their other goals, an emotion influences the person's frame of mind. Angry people lash out at others and may find it difficult to keep that emotion in check. Depression will make everything more difficult to do since the person is struggling to do anything at all.

- Crisis of Faith is an emotional conflict where the person struggles with their belief in God, or perhaps even in an idea like the inherent goodness of parents.

- Morality is an emotional conflict where the person struggles with the concepts of right and wrong. Is it alright for them to want what they want? Is it acceptable to do what they have planned to do in order to get what they want? Are the actions of someone else good, or evil, and what should they do about it?

- Self-Concept is an emotional conflict where the person struggles to find value within themselves. Does the person deserve the love of their fiancé? Does the person deserve to take over his brother's spot in the family business after his death in the war?

141

Example:

> *Robert Harrington and his wife, Mary Pratt, only had one child. They adopted Chester Williams from Robert's uncle when Chester's mom died. A story about the events surrounding Chester's adoption and his life with the Harrington's would probably include a crisis of faith prior to the adoption over whether Mary might ever become a mother, the struggles surrounding the decision to adopt, a conflict of emotions that involves grief for the death of Chester's mother, and Robert and Mary's joy about the adoption.*

Society – this is also known as Person vs. Society. What that means is the person is at odds with some segment of society. Obstacles in this category involve struggles that are part of a major difference in opinion.

- Government is bound to pass a law or start a war that upsets part of the population. Their actions will restrict what a person can do and might even outlaw what the person wants to do. Citizens can fight against the law and work to have it changed, they can work around the law or they can even thumb their noses at the rules and do what they want . . . with the risk of being fined or imprisoned. Then there's always the dangers of war and being drafted into a conflict.

- Religion is one of the greatest sources of conflict in the world with wars, heated debates, and prejudice. There's a good reason why people should never discuss religion and politics in polite company. Both topics can inspire strong opinions that trigger even stronger emotional response to whatever is said. If two religions exist where your story takes place, then there was plenty of conflict in that area.

- Social mindsets like dating someone in your own social class or the current set of rules for what's considered proper manners. Prejudice falls into this category. Every location and every period of time will have social expectations and anyone who fails to follow the rules of good behavior can expect plenty of conflict from society as a whole.

- Economic issues like layoffs or recessions have an effect on society. The Great Depression, the closing of manufacturing plants, or depleting the stockpile of a natural resource all have an impact on society. These events change how the nearby communities' function. And it doesn't have to be a negative outcome, the Gold Rush had a tremendous impact on the country.

- Social concepts like freedom, justice, equality, and morality can provide an especially powerful conflict. Did the person in your story have to face competition against bigger, stronger rivals? Did they compete for higher paying jobs against coworkers with better education or family connections to the boss? Did overwhelming debt limit the person's choices? Maybe the person wasn't the target of any of these concepts, but a crusader against what they felt were social injustices.

Example:

> *The Lindsay's emigrated from Ireland to escape religious persecution. As Protestants, they were treated as second-class citizens. Life was tough enough to begin with, then the added burdens of*

> *inequality made it worth the dangers of crossing the ocean and starting over on the American frontier. A story about William "The Immigrant" Lindsey would be sure to include plenty of obstacles due to religion, inequality, and economic hardships.*

Relationships – this isn't a separate category, but it may help to think of it as one. A relationship can result in both rivalry and emotional obstacles. How does the person's goal impact the lives of everyone around them? A decision to take a job in another city will affect the person's spouse and children, possibly the parents and siblings, as well as friends and neighbors. There's also a chance for conflict between all of these other people. A wife might resent a family friend for offering her husband a job in another city. Consider each of the relationships the person has and see if there is a conflict of interest for any of them and the goal.

THIS IS THE PRICE OF CONFLICT

After you decide what kind of obstacle stands in the person's way, determine how it hinders them from reaching the goal.

- Does the person need to move the obstacle out of the way before they can continue towards the goal? This could be a series of requirements a person must meet before they can work in their chosen career. Like lawyers needing to pass the bar exam. Or it could be a stubborn member of the board who needs to be convinced that the person's idea for a new product line will make the company a huge profit.

- Does the obstacle force the person to move around, over, or under the problem? This isn't limited to only physical actions. It can include attitudes and emotions. Perhaps the person had to learn how to work around a new city ordinance that affects their business. Or maybe it was simply a matter of a farmer using a different route to take his crops to town in order to avoid any trouble from an unfriendly neighbor.

- Is the obstacle a hazard that has the ability to harm the person? Like a wild animal, dangerous mountain terrain, or a group of rugged competitors who are not above attacking the person in order to stop him.

- Is the person lacking some ability or resource that they need to complete the goal?

- Does the obstacle force the person to work harder, longer, or at greater expense in order to obtain their goal?

- Does the obstacle require the person to find something before they can continue?

- Does the obstacle require the person to go to a specific place in order to obtain what they want?

These are just a few ideas on how an obstacle might hinder the person from getting what they want. Most of the problems an obstacle creates will be obvious when you stop and take a moment to think about them. Understanding how an obstacle prevents the person from obtaining their goal makes it easy to write about how they find a solution to the problem.

COMPLICATIONS

The more a person struggles to get what they want, the more interesting the story. We are instinctively drawn to stories where people face one difficulty after another in order to reach their goals.

Humans are hardwired to seek out examples of difficult challenges and the problem solving that results.

Increasing the difficulty of the challenges the person faces does more than rivet the reader's attention to the story. It also makes what the person wants more important. A goal that someone can reach in an afternoon is not nearly as important as one that takes years to accomplish with dozens of obstacles to overcome, which means the readers are all the happier when the person in the story finally succeeds.

Here are a few methods for making the person in the story struggle more.

- Keep adding complications. This is something all of us are familiar with. A series of complications turns a simple drive to the other side of town into an adventure. First you have to stop for gas but find that you left your wallet at home. Then you lock your keys in the car, two hours later, the locksmith has opened your car door and your gas tank is full, but you get a flat tire on the freeway. You pull off to the side and find that your spare tire is already on the car and a flat tire is in your trunk. Life is full of these kinds of complications.

- Raise the stakes. Show how it's more important for the person to get what they want than it was when they started the story. Maybe the great job the person wants is now the only job available. Or perhaps the house the person is supposed to inherit has been appraised at twice the amount everyone thought it was worth.

- Add another obstacle. This is a simple complication. Most goals have several steps involved to reach whatever it is the person wants. Just add those steps, one at a time, to increase the tension in the story. Make sure that all of the steps are real obstacles and not just minor inconveniences.

- Add another goal or requirement. This is a common complication in our lives. We start with a goal in mind and it changes as we learn more about the situation. A goal to graduate from medical school might change to graduating in the top 10% in order to get the job the person wants. Or perhaps the job the person wanted changes the requirement so that only the top 10% of the class now qualify, which now means more work and longer hours of study.

- Add another consequence if the person fails. What happens if the person doesn't get what they want? In the case of a person investing their life savings in a startup company, the consequence of failure is that they lose all of their money. But if the spouse has threatened to leave if the business fails, then we have added another consequence.

A variety of complications works best, include some small obstacles with the large ones. Show how the person overcomes some of the obstacles while they continue to struggle with the others. This creates an emotional rollercoaster that gives the reader a range of experiences, which is why rollercoasters have big and small drops as well as calm spots in between. These changes in pace give the people on the roller coaster a chance to catch their breath and it allows suspense to build as the coaster rolls toward the next big thrill.

Non-fiction stories will still need to stick to the facts, but any major event in a person's life is bound to have several obstacles that made it more difficult for them to get what they wanted. The methods above can make it easier to find the obstacles that actually existed. They are still a great way to bump up the level of tension in a non-fictional story. You just have to look for what really happened instead of making it up.

A FEW FINAL SUGGESTIONS

Make the stories active – have the person you're writing about do something. Don't have them stand around and let things happen. Action = tension. Whenever an obstacle appears in the story, have the person do something about it.

Change up the tension – use different types of tension and have those tensions come from different sources. You could mix emotional tension with a rivalry and throw in a little bit of romantic conflict. If your story is about the obstacles a person faces at work, toss in a couple of complications at home and a few with their friends. This prevents the story from feeling like there's too much of the same thing. People like variety and it helps if your story has a variety of problems.

Introduce change and uncertainty – most people dislike change because we don't know what to expect. We tend to dislike uncertainty for the same reason. Moving across the country or switching jobs are both situations that can leave us—and the reader—wondering what the future holds. Tension keeps people reading. If a couple has trouble getting pregnant and they try a new medical procedure to have a baby, then the reader will want to learn if it works. Uncertainty keeps people reading.

Make them suffer – pain, anguish, and other forms of suffering creates tension in a story. Alright, you won't actually be making anyone suffer—except the reader. This is about sharing the suffering the person in your story experienced in order to help others appreciate the trials they had to endure. The doubt and discomfort a person feel are an important part of their journey.

Interaction between people in the story is important – people are more likely than not to have a difference of opinion on something. Not only does that provide tension in a story, but it provides an opportunity for the reader to learn more about the people involved. As the people in the story interact, they will express their feelings, opinions, and character on whichever topic they are discussing. If you want readers to know that Grandpa was kind but stubborn, then have him interact with Grandma. That's sure to make the point.

NOTES

Randy Lindsay

NOTES

HOW TO BEGIN AND
END YOUR STORY

The beginning and the end of the story have been discussed to some extent in previous sections, but both are important and deserve a little extra attention. Beginnings can be hard to write and endings can be even more difficult to get right. The suggestions in this section are designed to help you fine tune both ends of your story.

BEGINNINGS

It's a challenge to decide where a story needs to start. Find the right moment and readers are immediately pulled into the details of the person's life and ready to discover more. Pick the wrong spot and readers may lose interest before the story really gets going.

The best place to start your story is at the moment when the events in the person's life apply to what you are writing about. If the story is about a person's entire life, then it's alright to start with their birth. A story about Grandma, Grandpa and their family could start with the first time they met, their first date, or even at their wedding. Even then, if the focus of the story is mostly on Grandma and Grandpa, then it makes more sense to start the story with how they met. Starting at their wedding works better if it's a story about the whole family.

You can also choose to start the story at the most interesting part of the person's life. Grandma and Grandpa might have a very funny story about when they started dating. That's an excellent way to begin a lighthearted story about their relationship. Or maybe you want the readers to know about the challenges the two of them faced together and the courage it took. In this situation, the tragic loss of one of their children at birth might be a better starting place. The starting point for your story really depends on what you want readers to know. Beginnings set the mood for the story. Choose a beginning that's appropriate for the mood you want.

STRONG STARTS

There are several elements that make the beginning of a story strong. The more of these that you can include in your story, the better your chances of hooking the reader.

1) Strong Opening Line – a great opening line is the best way to convince the reader that your story has potential. It can be funny. It can be poignant. It can make them wonder. Just make it powerful.

2) Strong Writing Style – this is not an element that is entirely under your control. Everyone is not blessed with the same level of talent. If you struggle to write, then do the best you can. Learn a few tips that will make your writing stronger. Focus more on the other elements of a strong beginning.

3) An Interesting Premise - this is about finding what is interesting in your story and then making sure the audience reads about it right away. It's been my experience that all events have something interesting about them.

4) Interesting People – people, like events, each have something interesting about them. It's just a matter of focusing on those quirky, endearing, or otherwise noteworthy traits and including them in the story.

5) An Unusual Starting Event – anything that makes for an amusing anecdote will work as an unusual starting event. Search for an often-told story about the person and see if you can turn that into your starting event.

6) Strong Setting – a good story has enough details to make the reader feel as if they are part of the events. Include plenty of colors, sounds, smells, textures, and items from the time and place of the story.

7) Conflict/Tension – nothing draws a crowd like conflict. Arguments, mental and physical challenges, and even the obvious fist fight not only grabs the reader's attention, but adds action and excitement to the story.

Write the beginning of your story and then go back and look for each of these elements. If any of them are missing, see if there is a way to add them to what you've already written. Even experienced writers have difficulty with writing a strong beginning to their story. Don't be discouraged if you have problems including these elements. This is a talent that takes practice.

Look at the start of your story. Look at this list. See if anything comes to mind that you can add. If it doesn't . . . don't worry about it. Try again next time. The purpose of this book is to make it as easy as possible to write better stories. Not to frustrate you.

BACKSTORY

There's a tendency for people to tell an audience what happened before a story began. This is known in the writing industry as backstory. It's natural to want to do this because those previous events have an impact on the story as it moves forward.

But don't do it. At least, don't cram twenty years of previous events into the first two pages of your story. If those events are important, wait until they become important to the story before you tell the reader about it. And there's a few reasons for this.

1) Including too many facts about the person, place, or what-have-you takes the reader out of the moment and slows the pace. Imagine that you write an amazing first paragraph that has your reader mesmerized. Then you write about the date and place the person was born, why his parents moved to the town where they live, and how many children they will eventually have later in the story. Now, the excitement you created in the first paragraph is gone.

2) Keeping any backstory close to the event where it's important makes it easier to connect the two together. If the person in your story had a nasty accident as a youth, then mentioning it just before they attempt a dangerous maneuver will create tension in the story. The reader will worry if the person will succeed or get hurt based on the event from the past.

3) Backstory tells the reader what happened, but a good story takes the reader through the experience. Show your readers what happens, don't tell them about it. Telling reduces any tension that might be a part of an event or situation.

ENDINGS

For the most part, readers judge a story by the way it ends. Even if you have no hopes of publishing your story to the general public, you probably still want friends and family to have a positive experience while reading about the person in your story.

There are several great ways to end a story. None of them are better or worse than the others. It's a matter of picking one that feels right to you and works for the story you are currently writing. It's entirely possible that if you wrote six stories that you might end each one of them in a different way.

Full Circle – a story with this kind of finish, ends where it began. That doesn't mean it has to start and end in the same place. The person in the story might find themselves in the same situation. Or in the same situation, but from a different position or point of view. It can also mean that the person in the story finds themselves at the beginning of another life journey that has some similarity to the one they just finished. For example:

- The story starts with the person walking down the main street of a small town. They leave to find opportunities in bigger and more exotic places. Eventually, the person returns home, and the story ends with them walking down the same street, but with a much different perspective.

- The start and end don't have to be about a place, it could be an activity, or a speech; like cooking with their mother and then cooking with their children, or the person's father giving a lecture on not throwing a ball in the house and ending the story with them giving the same speech to their children.

- The story starts with a problem. Maybe the person is inventing a machine that will change the way an industry works. The person succeeds at the end, but decides another part of the industry needs fixing as well. Boom. They're off on another adventure.

This is a powerful way to end a story because it provides a chance to show how the person has changed. If the person was stubborn and headstrong at the beginning of the story, show how they handle the same situation in a more understanding manner. Show the reader what the person learned on their journey through the story.

Relevant Quote – this kind of finish can be used with one of the other endings. In fact, it will be more powerful if you do. But if you really struggle with endings you could just slap on a relevant quote and be done with it. The story still needs to have an end point where all the questions are answered, all the problems addressed, and all the situations finished. Then find a quote that sums up your thoughts on the story and slap it on the last page.

For example, I could have used a quote to reinforce the message at the end of my memoir: *It doesn't matter how it happens. People make mistakes. All of us have flaws. What matters is that we are family . . . and family rocks. It is the love we share that makes us family.*

"Family is not an important thing. It's everything." – Michael J. Fox[5]

If you choose to use a quote, make sure it's cited well for copyright purposes.

- Make sure the quote is surrounded by quotation marks.

- List the original author. The person who wrote or spoke the quote.

- Make sure the text is identical to the original quote.

Connect Back – this kind of ending is similar to the Full Circle end. The difference is that the ending doesn't have to connect to the beginning of the story or repeat the event from a different frame of mind. It doesn't even have to show how the person has changed. This kind of ending is meant to remind us of some odd or offbeat event that happened earlier in the story. It can even be an event or situation that shows us that some things don't change. For example:

- A person in the story keeps losing their luggage at the airport. The situation has nothing to do with the story's message, but it gives the reader a sense that things continue. It also reminds the reader of one of the good parts of the story.

- A person struggles with their diet throughout the story, passing one pizza place after another in the hopes of losing weight. Then in the end, the person passes the most amazing pizza spot of all time and decides to go in for a slice . . . not an entire pie.

---

5 "Michael J. Fox Quotes." BrainyQuote.com. Brainy Media Inc, 2021. 17 February 2021. https://www.brainyquote.com/quotes/michael_j_fox_189302

The Epilogue – this is a popular end for many movies. The events related to the specific story have reached an end, but the lives of the people continue. A short mention of each person and what happens to them in the future is given. Like the story of a bunch of high school friends ends by telling the reader that the unruly troublemaker grows up to become a teacher. Or that the Prom Queen eventually becomes the First Lady.

As with all of the endings, the important elements of the story need to be over. All questions must be answered, all problems must be addressed, and all situations must be finished.

For example:

> *My grandmother lived a long life. At the age of 85, cancer struck again. It was mercifully swift and she died within weeks of the diagnosis. Mom was once again by her side. That's where she was for all of her family. Her only brother died of a heart attack in 1989. Their baby sister died in 2009. And Mom's closest friend, her sister Sharon, died in 2017. Both of her sisters taken away by the same illness that claimed their mother. Now, only Mom remains.*

The Philosopher – this kind of ending is an invitation to wonder. It might be a matter of wanting to know what will happen next. Or it could be the classic, "What if things had turned out differently?" This is a great way to include whatever thoughts the writer may have about the story. And if the story happens to naturally have some unanswered questions, then this is a good way to include them, leaving the reader wondering the same things as the writer.

For example, here are a few things I wondered as I wrote my memoir:

- ✐ Did my mother really not remember my biological father?

- ✐ What would my life have been like if my mother had married my biological father and moved to New Jersey?

- ✐ Will I eventually find out that I have a child I don't know about now?

Journey's End – this is a great ending for stories that represent a journey or a quest. The person reaches a destination (whether physical or metaphorical), a mystery is solved, or a secret is revealed. It works best when the actual end of the journey is the last section of the story.

For example:

> *David McCord died in 1819. After being captured by Indians during the French and Indian War, fighting in the Revolutionary War, and because of his experience with the Indians serving as a scout during the War of 1812 . . . David was killed by a group of Indians at his home in Williamson County, Tennessee.*

Lesson Learned – a story with this kind of ending has the person in the story, or even the narrator (the person writing the story) explain what was learned from the experiences that took place. It's perfectly fine to write from the point of view of the person in the story and then end with a few comments from you as the author.

For example:

> *I learned a lot from my father. He lived a rugged John Wayne kind of life, but encouraged me to write. To follow my heart and do what I thought was right for me. When other members of my family made fun of me for being a writer, my dad was my number one fan. Thanks, Dad. Thanks for having faith in me.*

Life Goes On - this is about showing that even as one story ends, another begins. Life goes on. The reader has a sense that the story is never truly over . . . and it isn't. The end of any story is really just the end of that chapter of life on Earth. An ending like this introduces the next project the person might attempt or someone from the next generation who will be carrying on the family traditions. This is also great if you are only doing a segment of a person's life or a section of the family. The introduction that ends the story is a hint to what happens next.

For example:

> *I turned the last page of my book. There were no more pages to review. No more corrections to make. I was done with my memoir. As excited as I was to be done with the long, tiring process of writing, revising, and publishing a book . . . I was even more excited to start a new project. Tons of titles stared out at me from my "Idea File."*

> *But only one of the projects spoke to me. It was time to finish The Gathering series. I opened my writing program and typed, 'The Return.' Then I cracked my fingers and started writing.*

BEFORE YOU WRITE "THE END"

Here's a few suggestions to make your ending the best it can be.

Make It Clear – Take extra effort to make sure the reader knows how the story ends. A line that indicates the person in the story never saw Uncle Billy again can be confusing. Did Uncle Billy die? Did he stop visiting the family on holidays? Or was he sent to prison? And be clear about whatever message you have for the reader. If you want people to know during the course of the story, Grandpa redeemed himself in your eyes, then make that point clear. This is not the time to be poetic or mysterious. Write your ending and then ask someone to read it. Did they understand what you wrote in the way you meant it?

Loose Ends – Make sure you have taken care of any loose ends. Read through the story and take note of any questions that are asked or any time someone wonders about an event. Then be sure you let the reader know the answer. If someone in the story said they were going to do something, then show the reader what happened. Most important of all, the person in the story needs to have either succeeded or failed in all of the goals they had before them. Don't leave the reader wondering if Aunt Mary ever made it to California or if your youngest son ever got the bike he wanted.

Ask yourself, "Were all the questions are answered, were all the problems addressed, and were all the situations finished?"

Stay Focused – Even though you are at the end, this is still the story for the person you are writing about. What did they learn? How did the obstacles that stood in the way make them the person they are now? What thoughts are going through their head? How do they feel about the journey that just ended?

Last Lines Matter – Pure and simple, the last line of a story matters. It's the punchline of the entire story. Take a little extra time to see if you can think of exactly the right thing to write. Do you want to end the story on a happy, uplifting note? Do you want to end it with a laugh? Maybe you have one last, important lesson to tell the reader. I know that I did.

This is the last paragraph from my memoir, *The Milkman's Son*,

> *It doesn't matter how it happens. People make mistakes. All of us have flaws. What matters is that we are family . . . and family rocks. It is the love we share that makes us family.*

ONE LAST WORD

Memoirs and family stories have great potential to enrich the lives of others. They also have the ability to cause devastating harm to the individuals you are writing about. Please, keep in mind, you can tell a story without including every detail of what happened. Some events are best left untold and the decision about what to include and what to leave private is probably the hardest part of writing a true story.

In *The Milkman's Son*, I made the decision to leave my mother out of the story as much as possible. Even though I received a lot of criticism for not having more of my memoir focused on her part of what happened . . . I know I did the right thing. I love my mother and did not want to hurt her. Instead, I wrote an author note to the readers, reminding them that this was a story about me and my two dads. If I was given a chance to do it over, I would make the same choice every time. Be careful with your words. Family is too important to lose to a careless remark.

NOTES

NOTES

FAMILY HISTORY WRITING CLUBS

Chances are good that, as you researched your family history, you reached out to other researchers for assistance. They may have done more research on a family line that you're just beginning. They might have more experience in a specific kind of record research. Or they know a few tricks about where to look for information that others often miss. Just as working with others can make the research process easier and more effective, forming a family history writing club can help make your stories better.

WRITING CLUB BENEFITS

Authors have been taking advantage of writing clubs for a long time. Except, writers refer to them as "critique groups" instead of writing clubs. The reason that writing groups are so popular is because they work. Meeting with like-minded people to discuss family history stories have several benefits.

Accountability – Knowing that you have a meeting and are expected to share a part of your story gives you extra incentive to write. It's amazing how well this works. Whether it's a matter of a deadline or that you simply don't want to disappoint the rest of the group, the commitment to have something ready makes it easier to motivate yourself to sit down and write.

Feedback – It can be difficult to find problems in your own work. Sometimes it's a case of being too close to your writing to see what's wrong. That's why it's helpful to have others read what you write. Some may have a better eye for grammar. Others may have a stronger feel for story structure. And sometimes it's just a matter that someone other than yourself is reading it. A writer might read their own work a dozen times and never find a problem, and then have someone else take a look at the story and find several mistakes.

Better Feedback – Not only will the members of your FH writing club give you feedback on your stories, the suggestions they make are likely to be better than the ones you receive from friends and family. Think back to all those pictures you drew in grade school. Most likely, when you brought those hard to decipher pictures home, your parents raved about how good they were. They were wanting to encourage you to keep drawing and get better.

The second reason the feedback from your group will probably be better is that they have more experience with writing family history stories. At least they will once they've written a few stories themselves and sat through a couple of writing club meetings. Because the members of the writing club spend more time writing than the average person, they tend to be better judges of what your story needs.

Support – Writing can be a frustrating task. Members of your family history club know what it's like to try to turn the facts and statistics of a person's life into a story that people will want to read. At times, it will be a comfort to be surrounded by others who understand the challenges you face as a family history writer.

Fun – FH writing clubs are fun. This is your chance to sit around and talk with people who have the same passion as you. You'll be hard pressed to find anyone outside the writing club that is going to find the challenges and discoveries of family history writing as interesting as they do.

GIVING CRITIQUES

When you read someone else's story and provide meaningful feedback, that's known as a critique. The interesting thing about critiquing another writer's story is that as you practice looking for problems in a story, it trains you to be a better writer. You will start noticing some of the same problems in your own writing.

But before you run off with red pen in hand, anxious to slash your way through the writing club's stories, here's a few tips:

- Be kind. A writing club is about helping others improve their story. It's not about making them feel as if their writing is horrible and they should give up.

- Respect their style. Everyone has their own style of writing. It's alright if the words other writers use and the way they put them together is different from your own. Suggestions like, "It would sound better if you wrote it this way," are best saved for sentences that are awkward and hard to read.

- Identify the problem and offer a solution. Although it can be helpful to point out a problem in a story, it's better if you can explain exactly how and why it needs to be changed. Maybe a paragraph has a lot of passive language that can be improved by making it more active.

- Recognize that it's their story. Make your suggestions and then leave it up to the person to use them as they feel is appropriate.

Many critique groups use what is known as the "Sandwich Method" for giving advice on another writer's story. This is meant to keep the comments helpful while limiting the amount of hurt feelings. It can be tough to hear that the words you so carefully wrote need to be changed . . . or even deleted.

1) What works. Mention the parts of the story that are easy to understand and entertaining. Explain why those parts work as well as they do.

2) How it can be improved. This is where you share your constructive feedback on the story. Focus on identifiable problems, like grammar, inconsistencies, sentences that are hard to read, and which parts of the story may have dragged a little.

3) End on a positive note. The best way to do this is to tell the person what you liked best about the story. Point out any lines or events that really grabbed your interest.

RECEIVING CRITIQUES

For many, this is the hardest part of writing a story. It's easy to feel as if the members of your writing club are attacking you personally. But that isn't the case. The main reason for participating in a writing club is to make your stories as good as possible. Here's a few suggestions on how to get the most out of the feedback you receive.

Don't take it personally – The comments from members of the writing club are not about you. Every professional writer I know has a group who look for problems in their stories. Embrace the opportunity to fix something you missed. Rejoice that other members of your writing club are stronger in some areas than you and they are sharing their talent to improve your story. Or just bite your lip and accept that progress is sometimes uncomfortable.

Give it a chance – If a comment bothers you, set it aside and come back to it. See if the suggestions that were made make sense and can improve your story. Look for how the comment might lead to new ideas that will make the story even better than it is now.

Remain true to yourself – Realize that nobody knows your story better than you. Stay true to your style and true to the story. Sometimes that means you have to ignore a suggestion because it isn't right for your story. That doesn't mean you should reject all suggestions because, "They just don't understand my artistic vision." Many of the comments will offer excellent ways to improve what you wrote.

STARTING A FH WRITING CLUB

If you can't find a family history writing club, you may have to start one yourself. No problem. It's easy to do. Just follow the steps below.

1) Locate others who are interested in writing memoirs or family histories. Ask your friends and members of the family and see if they would like to help preserve the history of your ancestors. Connect with members of a family history research group and ask them to join you. Search Facebook, Twitter, and other social media outlets for groups that share the same research interests. Ask a bunch of your friends. Post a notice at your local library, stating that you want to start a new group. You can also search MeetUp for groups that already exist.

* When searching on Facebook and Twitter, try using the following hashtags: #writingcommuinty, #critiquegroup, and #critiquepartner.

2) Limit the group. The more people you have in the group, the longer it takes for feedback and can be difficult to manage. My experience is that 3-5 people is the best size for a group.

3) Online or in person? Decide whether the group will meet in person or exchange feedback electronically. Both methods have their advantages and drawbacks.

4) Meet on a regular basis. Whether you meet every week, every two weeks, or once a month, make sure you have a regular schedule. Longer than once a month and you lose many of the benefits of a writing club.

5) Decide how much of your story to share. Between 2 to 10 pages works best for most groups, but will depend on the number of people and the amount of time you have for sharing. You can even share a complete story if it's fairly

short. Online groups can share more pages because they are not limited to the time set aside for a meeting.

6) Decide on a group format. There are several ways to share stories and receive comments. Everyone in the club can email what they want to share with the others and then during the meeting, each person has a chance to offer suggestions. Or each person can read what they want to share and then ask for comments from the rest of the group. Whoever is sharing will need to decide how much of their time goes to reading and how much is for comments.

7) Decide on the club rules. Are there any kind of stories the club doesn't want shared? Stories that might be too violent or too sad. What kind of suggestions does everyone in the group think are appropriate? Can the person decide how serious they want the suggestions? Maybe your writing club wants to start each meeting with an inspirational quote. You might even decide to have a rotating assignment to bring treats.

That's it! Now, you can start on that memoir or family story you've been wanting to write. And if you're wondering, "How am I going to remember all of this?"

There's no need to worry. It takes time to learn writing skills. No one should expect to master all of these concepts overnight. Pick one of the ideas that excites you and work on that. If you liked how historic facts can be turned into interesting story details, then work on that. Practice that activity. Then when you feel comfortable with that skill . . . try another one.

Keep this book handy as a reference guide. You won't need to read every page again. Just look through the bullet points to remind you of ideas you've already learned. Or go straight to the section you want to focus on and read the parts that will help with your current story.

The great thing about reading this book is that the methods you've already learned from it will make the stories you're writing better. You already have ideas on what to do to improve your memoir or family story. The more you study and practice the suggestions in this book, the more your writing will improve.

Congratulations.

See, what did I tell you? Easy-Peasy.

And if you have any questions, contact me at:

easypeasymethod@gmail.com

WHAT NEXT?

After all that work, what are you going to do with your story? Typing the words "The End" on the last page doesn't mean you're finished. It's just means you're ready for the next step. *Publishing.*

Are you going to share it with the whole world, or just with family and friends? What is your plan to publish your story? Are you going to self-publish? Are you looking for someone to help you? If you want to publish and market your book, where do you even start?

As a budding writer, your world has just blossomed into a multitude of paths. You might want to turn your family story into an epic novel.

All your creativity will remain in the dark if you don't have an outlet to expand your audience.

Signup for my free training, "The Three Sentence Story," and get access to lots of good content to improve your writing skills and help you to build your own tribe of fans, anxiously waiting for your next book.

www.TheThreeSentenceStory.com

I invite you to subscribe to my podcast called "Something Worth Writing," where I explore a variety of writing methods, styles and techniques that can help you improve your craft.

www.SoundCloud.com/Something-Worth-Writing

ABOUT THE AUTHOR

RANDY LINDSAY is a native of Arizona. He lives in Mesa with his wife, five of this nine children, a dog, a cat, and a hyper-active imagination. His wife calls him the "Story Man" because he sees everything as material for a story.

The Easy-Peasy Method for Writing Memoirs and Family Stories is Randy's eighth book. After writing six fiction titles, Randy made a shocking personal discovery and wrote his memoir, The Milkman's Son. Reader response to his story convinced him to switch to non-fiction writing in order to help others to share their amazing stories with the world.

Randy teaches storytelling at writing conferences, local libraries, and family history groups. He judges beginning of book contests, hosted the Ready-Set-Write podcast, hosted the So You Think You Can Write show on YouTube, and currently hosts the Something Worth Writing podcast.

Ready Set Write Podcast
http://www.readysetwritepodcast.com/

So You Think You Can Write
https://bit.ly/38t3XYM

Something Worth Writing Podcast
www.SoundCloud.com/Something-Worth-Writing

THE MILKMAN'S SON
BY RANDY LINDSAY

Available in Hardcover, Ebook, and Audio Book.

Raised in a family he bore little resemblance to Randy was jokingly referred to as "the Milkman's Son." This warm and candid memoir chronicles the unraveling of a family secret, which begins with Randy's dad having dreams about deceased relatives urging him to complete their family tree. Randy agrees to help with the genealogy, but after his searching leads to a dead end, he takes a commercially available DNA test. The results reveal a possible genetic match to a sister, which begins a familial quest that forever changes the author's life.

Featuring a cast of vivid characters richly drawn from two distinct families, The Milkman's Son reveals on man's family tree, pulling back layers of new information as he gets closer to the truth about a biological father, siblings, and family members he never knew about.

177

This is a story about accepting, forgiving, reuniting, and, most importantly, it's about the bonds that connect us and the unconditional love that makes us feel like we belong.

"The Milkman's Son takes readers on a journey with emotional twists and turns as Lindsay learns about and uses many new research tools available, including DNA testing." – Cindy Williams, The Arizona Beehive

"Recommended for fans of family memoirs, and especially for readers with an interest in genealogy." – Library Journal

"Lindsay's memoir is truly a work of our times in the way it shows how internet ancestry sites and crowd-sourced research come together with readily accessible DNA kits to help us know who we are and where we come from." – Shoba Viswanathan, Booklist

Get your copy of Milkman's Son at bit.ly/milkmansson

www.ingramcontent.com/pod-product-compliance
Lightning Source LLC
Chambersburg PA
CBHW060454280326
41933CB00014B/2752